# A HAPPY FUTURE IS A
# THING OF THE PAST

## FIELD NOTES

SERIES EDITOR: Paul Mattick

A series of books providing in-depth analyses of today's global turmoil as it unfolds. Each book focuses on an important feature of our present-day economic, political and cultural condition, addressing local and international issues. 'Field Notes' examines the many dimensions of today's social predicament and provides a radical, politically and critically engaged voice to global debates.

Published in association with the *Brooklyn Rail*

Titles in the series:

# A HAPPY FUTURE IS A THING OF THE PAST

*The Greek Crisis and Other Disasters*

PAVLOS ROUFOS

REAKTION BOOKS

*For En, Alva and Nikolai, without whom nothing.*

Published by Reaktion Books Ltd
Unit 32, Waterside
44–48 Wharf Road
London N1 7UX, UK
www.reaktionbooks.co.uk

First published 2018

Printed and bound in Great Britain by TJ International, Padstow, Cornwall

A catalogue record for this book is available from the British Library

ISBN 978 1 78023 985 9

# Contents

# Introduction

In May 2017 representatives of the Troika (European Commission, European Central Bank, International Monetary Fund) and of the Greek government of Syriza/Independent Greeks (ANEL) met to put the final touches to yet another set of austerity measures heralded as 'necessary structural reforms'. An agreement was reached and the reforms were formalized with a 'Supplemental Memorandum of Understanding' (MOU), essentially updating reform commitments undertaken in 2015. The measures demanded in exchange for another bail-out were not simply unreasonable: the Greek economy is expected in the agreement to run a primary surplus budget of 3.5 per cent of GDP per year until 2022, a level never achieved by *any* government, let alone one decimated by a near decade-long recession. Public debt, presented as a key determinant of Greece's dire economic situation and, therefore, the supposed main target of the restructuring process, has been steadily increasing, but debt restructuring remains outside the scope of the negotiations. If Greece abides by the structural adjustment programme (and if its projections are not as wrong as all previous ones), its debt will be repaid in 2059. Until that time the debt remains unsustainable, something already recognized by one of the key creditors behind the bail-out, the International Monetary Fund (IMF).[1]

In the course of the last eight years, during which Greece's social, political and economic conditions have been irreversibly transformed and worsened, one thing has remained constant: the idea that continued austerity remains the only possible path if Greece wants to avoid an even worse fate. Despite official statements (more or less identical to each other since 2010), hardly anyone even pretends anymore that the reforms undertaken will restore growth or economic viability. If the MOU's signed so far targeted four main areas of economic activity (debt sustainability, the modernization of the state mechanism, growth/competitiveness through reduced labour costs and bank stability), they have only succeeded in keeping the insolvent Greek banks afloat and radically lowering labour costs.

The obvious and dramatic failure of austerity in all other areas continues to be treated, by those responsible, as somehow irrelevant even though their own figures easily illuminate this implosion: since 2010 unemployment has almost doubled from 12.2 per cent to 20.6 per cent (Eurostat, October 2017); GDP has contracted by more than 25 per cent, while the debt/GDP ratio has increased from 126.8 per cent to a staggering 176.8 per cent (Eurostat, October 2017); the collapse of demand has brought the economy to its knees through a steady deflationary path, while the amount of capital destruction is equivalent to that of France or Italy after the Second World War. Unfortunately, translating the real impact of these dramatic figures on people's lives has proven elusive. Perhaps a more direct example will help.

Marina is 37 years old. Her parents lived in their own flat and ran a small business, while Marina's temporary contract in the public sector was made permanent in 2007. As a result, she earned a decent income of 1,100 euros per month, allowing her to rent her own small flat. Prompted by the sense of security that came from a tenured public sector job, her parents' earnings and their property as collateral, Marina decided in 2008 to take out a loan to buy her own house.

Since the crisis of 2010 Marina's world has been shattered. In these last seven years, she has lost more than 40 per cent of her income, while her parents have seen their income reduced by 50 per cent, as demand has collapsed. Owning property has become a veritable curse, as the property tax has increased more than eightfold since 2011. Although real estate prices have fallen by more than 50 per cent, it remains extremely difficult to sell one's property at a reasonable price.[2] Due to the cuts in her wages (and her parents' income), Marina was unable to keep up with her loan repayment. She has lost the house, but not her debt. In 2017, reflecting the near collapse of the Greek healthcare system, Marina's father died from a cancer that could have been treated had it been detected in time. The public hospital he attended no longer had the equipment for such tests.

Marina's story is indicative for one simple reason: her situation portrayed, if not the average Greek family, then the *ideal* of every average Greek family. This lower-middle-class experience (a tenured job in the public sector, a small-sized business, home ownership) represented the closest thing to a comfortable life as conceived in pre-crisis Greece. No one in Marina's position could even pretend that this is still the case today. I leave it to the reader to imagine what the economic collapse of the last eight years has meant to people who did not share Marina's 'privileged' life.

The failure of crisis management of Greece since 2010 has been repeatedly predicted, not merely by the critics of the programmes, but by its designers too. A representative of the IMF (protected by anonymity) declared as much in October 2016 when he confessed a simple truth: that the economic situation of Greece is 'beyond repair'.

The question begs itself: a set of policies doomed to fail in achieving their official goal must, assuming the sanity of its makers, have some other, perhaps unspoken, aim. Excuses such as mistakes in technocratic calculations, an underestimation of the effects of ceaseless recession or the insistence that structural reforms have not yet been fully implemented, have long lost their ability to convince. This book aims to illuminate the key coordinates of the Greek crisis and its management and provide an answer to this central question.

Until today, commentators on the Greek crisis and its governance are roughly split between two categories: those who primarily focus on elucidating the chronic pathogenies of the Greek economy and society, and those who mostly concentrate on the international framework.[3] The first, intentionally or not, facilitate the dominant narrative that sees the outbreak of the crisis as a result of Greeks wildly overspending, forever unable to modernize/rationalize their corrupt state mechanism and somehow deserving their regrettable fate. The second category, despite its possible merit in outlining the international context, tends to ignore specific particularities of the Greek formation. What this approach fails to understand is not so much the origins of the crisis (which are, of course, not to be found within Greece) but the precise reasons why the management of the crisis has produced the results it has.

The purpose of this book is to go beyond this dichotomy to offer a critical look at the political economy of the Greek crisis, through a temporal and geographical widening of scope: the historical development of the Greek economy, politics and society; the international context within which it is firmly situated; and the conflicts that emerged in respect to the handling of the crisis. Maybe then the exact reasons why a happy future is today considered a thing of the past will become clearer.

*one*

# A Thing of the Past

The immense destruction of productive capacity during the Second World War was the foundation upon which the u.s. became the economic hegemon of the world. In 1944 the u.s. initiated the Bretton Woods Agreement, a system of fixed exchange rates that would allow the free convertibility of currencies as a key structure of international trade. The catch was that, with the formal excuse of avoiding the competitive devaluations seen as partly responsible for the 1930s depression, all parties to the Bretton Woods club agreed to peg their currencies to the (undervalued) u.s. dollar, set at $35 per ounce of gold. The Bretton Woods system marked the onset of the dollar's hegemony as the de facto currency of international trade. As Henry C. K. Liu has succinctly written, this meant that 'the u.s. produce[d] dollars and the rest of the world produce[d] things that dollars could buy'. Under this arrangement,

> the world's interlinked economies no longer trade to capture a comparative advantage; they compete in exports to capture needed dollars to service dollar-denominated foreign debts and to accumulate dollar reserves to sustain the exchange value of their domestic currencies. To prevent speculative and manipulative attacks on their currencies, the world's central banks must acquire and hold dollar reserves

in corresponding amounts to their currencies in circulation. The higher the market pressure to devalue a particular currency, the more dollar reserves its central bank must hold. This creates a built-in support for a strong dollar that in turn forces the world's central banks to acquire and hold more dollar reserves, making it stronger.[1]

Despite its international scope, the Bretton Woods Agreement was embedded with specific barriers to the movement of capital across borders (seeking to restrict speculative flights and enhance currency defence). Post-war financial flows were dominated by inter-governmental loans and foreign direct investments (FDI), focusing on capital accumulation and growth within a framework of relatively fixed exchange rates and monetary policy control, at the expense of establishing certain limitations on the free movement of capital.

The limits placed on financial speculation allowed for low domestic interest rates, something that facilitated the ability of governments to fund large-scale infrastructural projects and domestic welfare. The widespread adoption of the Fordist organization of the production process, which enhanced labour productivity and contributed to the mass production of commodities at affordable prices; the increased labour migration from the global South to the North; and the crucial social consensus for putting a cap on labour militancy in exchange for democratic integration and consumption: all these created the framework within which Keynesian monetary and fiscal policies of deficit spending, moderate inflation and full employment were expanded.

To accommodate the above developments in the landscape of post-war Europe, while also strengthening an economic defence umbrella in opposition to the Soviet world, the U.S. initiated the Marshall Plan, a massive programme of economic assistance to Europe that would allow the latter both to regenerate its productive capacity and to import u.s. products. The significant economic outputs and capital accumulation that Western European countries achieved (with West Germany being the primary example) through the increased degree of economic collaboration among European nations strengthened the idea that further economic integration would further facilitate growth. But there were exceptions.

## Marshall's Bombs

Greece emerged from the Second World War in a state of economic ruin. Despite the immediate loans and economic assistance (at first from the British in 1946, and then with the Marshall Plan in 1947), it would take another decade for any signs of economic recovery to appear. In the immediate post-war period, the economy was plagued with constant depreciations of the currency, a flourishing black market, the inability of the central bank to enforce the drachma (with people putting more trust in the British pound or gold) and minimal industrial activity. It was not until 1953 (when a final depreciation equated the drachma to its black market price) that a more rigorous attempt at fiscal policy and balancing the budget allowed the economy to start picking up its pace.

Prior to that, the social and political outcome of the war had rendered economic decisions secondary in comparison to the reality of civil war. If the Marshall Plan was key to the reconstruction of the European economy, its arrival in Greece carried slightly different historical weight. In fact, for a very large part of the population who belonged or sympathized with the de facto military victor of the end of the war, elas,[2] the Marshall Plan meant nothing but napalm bombs, ideological coercion, the protection of Nazi collaborators, a violent uprooting of the countryside and its inhabitants, exile and prison.

The end of the Second World War had raised the question of the legitimization of the post-war order. For Greece, in particular, this issue was crucial: the official state apparatus (police, army and so on) had lost its legitimacy after openly collaborating with the occupying forces, their authority further undermined by EAM's ability to create a parallel state mechanism, particularly present in places that the (pre-war) state had left outside of its scope of influence, such as the almost-uninhabitable mountainous regions. When the Nazis left Greece, the power vacuum was violently fought over, with armed groups competing to impose their own legal and political rules. By the end of the civil war in 1949, it was the anti-communist Right, with the direct military and financial support of the British, that managed to impose their own will and establish the totalitarian post-war Greek democracy.

A crucial aspect of the U.S. post-war economic stimulus was its intent, among other things, to counteract Soviet influence. This might help explain why, after the disastrous civil war, which only added to the already devastating effect of the occupation, Greek society was organized on the basis of a systematic exclusion and persecution of all those who had (directly or indirectly) provided KKE/EAM with their military and social base.[3] Apart from the thousands who ended up in prison or in exile, or were executed, those who remained 'free' were persistently denied access to the (in any case minimal) economic activity of the country. The result was a rather contradictory process, in which the massive exit from the countryside towards the urban centres (a deliberate state policy aimed at undermining the power base of the so-called 'communist gangs') coincided with an irrational and highly politicized allocation of the newly proletarianized population among the different forms of economic activity. In practice, it meant a minimal possibility of employment in the public sector, or in those parts of the private sector that had close ties to the state mechanism, for anyone associated (through fact, rumour or family ties) with the Left. For the majority of those who had fought alongside the Left for the liberation of Greece, aside from the injuries of prison time and exile, there was an added insult: only by publicly denouncing 'communism' (which, more often than not, meant their own history or families) could they hope for any breathing space in the asphyxiating environment of post-war Greece.[4]

## Working Relations

This predicament unfolded within the existing and rather peculiar structure of work relations in Greece, one characterized by an inflated self-employed sector, a low number of wage-workers, and a tight and complementary connection between family structures, such as small agricultural family units, and wage work. As various reports of the Bank of Greece of the period inform us, it was precisely this conjunction between family units and waged work that allowed for a constant downward pressure on wages, safe in the knowledge that the informal economy contributed directly to the reproduction of the workforce, thus relieving capital from the obligation to raise wages. But this was not all. The lack of a direct dependence on the wage form allowed the government to continue the policies of persecution and exclusion, as well as to favour unapologetically the often short-term immediate needs of private capital.

In this context, the Keynesian-influenced policies that were increasingly dominant across the West during that period never reached Greece. Wages were still seen merely as a cost and not an investment, while inflationary pressures did not lead to an increase in wages (and thus consumption) but rather to the constant reduction of purchasing power. As a result, a certain consolidation of an economic and social reality occurred. While the increase of labour productivity in Europe and the u.s. corresponded (with small statistical variations) to wage increases – a process compensated for, when necessary, by welfare and/or class struggles – in Greece the opposite was the case. Labour productivity was entirely disconnected from wages, while the persistence of close family ties and the informal economy (in mostly small agricultural units[5]) compensated for the scandalous absence of welfare supplements. Moreover the political climate automatically outlawed any direct expressions of class antagonism as signs of 'communist agitation', with tremendous legal and social consequences.

Throughout the 1950s successive governments and the Central Bank of Greece set out an economic policy focused on inviting foreign investments (by lowering taxation), relaxing trade tariffs and promoting exports (primarily of raw materials). At the same time, they tried to increase private capital investments through cheap credits, hoping eventually to reverse the trend of state-dominated investments, which burdened the deficit. In return, they maintained a labour power that was unskilled, cheap and unorganized, taking advantage of this specific competitive edge to raise productivity with a combination of investments in technology and a better organization of the production process. A contradictory situation started, nonetheless, to unfold: although continuous political repression and economic policy did its best to ensure that workers would remain low paid and unorganized, the same conditions forced workers to maintain their closely knit family ties, which, in turn, rendered them less dependent on the wage form and less mobile than what would have been profitable for capital.

In any case, the combination of all these elements made the proletarian experience particularly painful. Led by necessity, thousands of Greeks emigrated to wealthier European countries and beyond to the u.s. and Australia. And even though some sectors of private capital would complain about this systematic drain of labour power, mass migration was primarily recognized as a further opportunity to export social antagonism.[6]

In the early 1960s, with the Marshall Plan over and a large deficit in current accounts, state and private capital sought ways of realigning Greece with the 'miracle' of economic growth in the rest of Europe. For this reason they began negotiations to join the European Economic Community (EEC), which resulted in a 1961 agreement giving Greece the status of Associate Member of the Community. The main focus was the further relaxation of tariffs between Greece and EEC member-states, as well as an EEC promise to intervene on behalf of Greece in the European Investment Bank in order to finance investment plans in Greece. At the same time, the Central Bank began a programme for the creation of pro-industry committees and organizations, whose aim was to facilitate, promote and finance industrial activity.[7] Despite these efforts, the Greek government and its Central Bank still had a limited capacity to design monetary and fiscal policy, a result of their inability to convince the public to trust the drachma, the official currency, as opposed to foreign currencies or gold.[8]

Nonetheless, productivity increases (still disconnected from wages), low capital taxation, the export of class conflict and the substantial incomes transferred home by migrants allowed a certain growth and an improvement in economic performance, a fact reflected in the increase of industrial production as well as consumption, expanding the internal market.[9] These developments were also reflected in a relative political liberalization, which, to the detriment of the political and economic ruling class, brought to the fore a whole new pressure from below. Though they are often described as expressing demands for fairer political representation (the Left was still illegal at the time), along with a moral protest against corruption and social exclusion,[10] the struggles that broke out in the mid-1960s went deeper than that. And they sought to overturn the very conditions described in the opening of this paragraph.

Starting in 1964, strike activity in particular saw a massive increase, eventually forcing bosses to concede generous wage increases.[11] One could say that Greek workers were merely trying to catch up with the rest of Europe, forcing state and private capital to observe a closer connection between productivity and wages,[12] something that their European counterparts had already achieved. But the tolerance of the ruling class towards these drastic changes was short-lived.

In the turmoil that exploded, a series of failed governments started playing musical chairs, each one less able to control and contain the wave of strikes, riots and political upheaval. Quite crucially, the non-existence of trade unions or legal left-wing political parties (a predicament that had proved quite useful to capital up until that point) now became problematic, as there existed no mediators that could absorb the anger and channel demands into more acceptable paths. On 21 April 1967, as if directly responding to the mounting complaints of the capitalist class, army tanks rolled down the main streets of Athens. A small group of army colonels opted for a simple way to untie the Gordian knot produced by social antagonism and its dangerous political consequences: dictatorship.[13]

## The Politics of Plaster

The military dictatorship of 1967–74 focused as much as its democratic predecessors on promoting manufacture and industrial activity, on lowering tax expectations for investors and on boosting the tourist and construction sectors. It also tried to finance public works through more loans.[14] Another focus was the promotion and support of exports, which almost doubled (in size and profit) between 1967 and 1974. All this was made possible through the suppression of all workers' demands and mobilizations, thereby ensuring that wages would once again be disconnected from labour productivity.

The above mix created a semblance of economic growth in the dictatorships' early period, allowing the state to increase its credit towards the private sector. Unfortunately for them, however, the collapse of the Bretton Woods system in 1971 reversed these 'successes' and forced an 8 per cent devaluation of the drachma. This worsened the current accounts deficit even more and prices started to hike. In order to control them, the Central Bank postponed its provision of credit (especially towards construction), but the further devaluation of the dollar one year later forced the drachma to plunge another 10 per cent. With some delay, the Central Bank decided in 1973 to raise interest rates in order to contain liquidity but all their efforts proved fruitless, as the oil crisis forced a further decline of economic activity.[15]

By the end of 1973 the complete failure of the junta to provide growth or even economic stability outweighed its success in providing graveyard-like silence and social peace. The sense of an impending collapse was also reflected at a social level: in November of the same year, what started as a student uprising against the junta's tight grip on university politics ended up in a fierce and violent proletarian riot that the dictatorship was forced to suppress using army units, leaving many dead.[16] Soon after, in a misguided attempt to establish a puppet government in neighbouring Cyprus, the dictatorship played its last card and lost. The attempted coup in Cyprus led to the mobilization of the Turkish army, which invaded and split the island in two. The foreign allies of the dictatorship did not lift a finger and the dictatorship crumbled. Seeing an open door, right-wing politicians of the democratic camp rushed to fulfil the necessary role of controlled transition: their concern was to avoid the possibility that the experience of the 1973 violent uprising, coupled with the veritable collapse of the state mechanism in July 1974, might lead to unwanted and unstable situations – in other words, to some undesirable re-emergence of the Left.[17]

## Post-dictatorship Blues

The end of the dictatorship saw the beginning of a period of continual currency depreciations (in 1975, 1976 and 1977) that allowed for some mild recovery, coupled with an official application to rejoin the EEC as a full member in 1975, in an effort gradually to disentangle the drachma from the fluctuating dollar and connect it to European currencies. The aims of this new strategy were, among others, to control price increases, improve the current account balance and facilitate the economic recovery. It also led to important political developments.

Kostas Karamanlis, the founder of the conservative right-wing New Democracy party and three-times Prime Minister of Greece in the 1950s and early '60s, returned from self-exile and tried to balance a fragile political situation. His personality and charisma, as well as the fear of a return of the junta, were enough to win him 54.7 per cent of the vote in the first post-dictatorship elections of July 1974. As a result of the Cyprus/Turkey conflict, and under pressure from below due to U.S. involvement in the dictatorship, Karamanlis announced the withdrawal from NATO, a short-lived gesture but one with important symbolic relevance. His main aim was to try to balance a potential threat that was forming between an enthusiastic youth left-wing movement (inspired by the struggles against the junta) and a military apparatus not entirely convinced that it was ready to step out of the picture. It was not by chance that in his first speech to the Greek people on 25 July 1974, he specifically addressed these two categories.[18]

In terms of economic policy, Karamanlis attempted a delayed catch-up with the (almost defunct) Keynesian model of economic policy, which, in conjunction with the background of the Greek economy, translated as an attempt to expand the state sector. This Keynesian shift was confirmed by the early statements of Karamanlis's choice for head of the Central Bank, the seasoned banker Xenofon Zolotas.[19] General Government expenditures rose (from 28.4 per cent in 1974 to 38 per cent by 1981), while deficit spending was multiplied fivefold in the same period. And although of a right-wing disposition, Karamanlis also opted for a programme of nationalizations (Olympic Airways, Commercial Bank), prompting commentators of the period to talk of a 'social*ist*-mania' and a leading right-wing newspaper to ask, 'Mr Karamanlis, are you a communist?'

One of Karamanlis's main goals (and successes) was the inclusion of Greece in the EEC. The historic move was heralded as an attempt to bolster the democratic transition and Greece's bonds to the West; but the economic reality of the time meant that the Greek economy suddenly became even more exposed to global economic stagflation, as well as the consequences of the second oil crisis of 1978. As the EEC brought about an even further relaxation of protective tariffs, the international non-competitiveness of Greek capital was dramatically exposed and the downward spiral of the global economy took a heavy toll on Greece. Rising inflation (around 26 per cent in 1974), a GDP decrease (–6.4 per cent) and a decrease in agricultural and construction investments gradually made the initial enthusiasm for the transition to democracy evaporate. But the reactions to this economic decline were very different this time, reflecting the drastic changes of Greek society since the colonels' rule.

Already by the late 1960s the agricultural population had decreased, prompting further urbanization and an increase in the industrial and service-sector proletariat. The move away from the countryside had also reshaped family structures, reducing them to the smaller-sized nuclear form, a change that directly increased wage dependency. The resulting lack of a family structure to compensate for wage losses (put differently, the increased commodification of the reproduction of the working class) meant that the recession gave rise to fierce class struggles.

Their outbreak was also facilitated by a characteristic already noted in the social struggles of 1962–5: the historical absence of established mediating mechanisms such as trade unions or political parties, which have historically been able to control and channel demands. Instead, what took place in most workplaces was the formation of base unions – that is, working-class organizations or assemblies that were impromptu, largely autonomous and without official trade-union experience or recognition. These structures played a crucial role in organizing and defending a significant number of successful wildcat strikes, which placed proletarian interests above the wished-for 'national unity', as the deterioration of working conditions in favour of private capital was called. Though these base unions have not received enough attention in Greek historiography, their significance did not escape the attention of the capitalist class of the time. In a speech given at a conference of the Greek Industrialists' Union (SEB), one can catch a glimpse of the reasons capital recognized them as a threat, as well as a hint on how to defeat them:

> Base-unions within companies represent specific interests and face particular problems in given workplaces. The viewpoint of top-down unionism necessarily includes, on the other hand, not only conflicting and differential workers' interests but a macroeconomic surveillance of the conditions within which these interests exist. This divergence causes by its nature conflicting relations, which have been exacerbated by the inability of traditional unionism to integrate this new phenomenon of base-unions . . . The result of this phenomenon is the centrifugal behaviour of the [workers'] base, which assigns visible characteristics of indeterminacy in small scale work relations and causes obstructions to the programming ability of companies.[20]

This explosion of social antagonism was, naturally, met with direct state repression.[21] But in the same way that laissez-faire capitalism cannot stop a riot, police repression cannot, in itself, reconfigure economic coordinates. The legalization of left-wing political parties (especially KKE) and their engagement in trade unions that were, until that moment, under the direct control of the bosses was gradually recognized as unavoidable for imposing a sense of sober and responsible mediation on unruly workers. Eventually it was the combined effort of internal and external repression of the wildcat struggles that managed to halt their increase as late as 1978, though their gains lasted even longer, as indicated by the fact that wage increases greatly surpassed productivity rates throughout the whole period. In order to put a stop to the slowdown of economic activity and the loss of profits, a deeper transformation was required. A new social contract that could combine economic growth and increased government spending *as well as* a systematic recuperation of social conflicts needed to be signed. And there was no political party in Greece that could deliver such a historical task other than the Panhellenic Socialist Movement (PASOK).

*two*

# The Monetarist Transformation

We used to think that you could spend your way out of a recession,
and increase employment by cutting taxes and boosting government
spending. I tell you in all candour that that option no longer exists,
and that in so far as it ever did exist, it only worked, on each
occasion, since the war, by injecting a bigger dose of inflation
into the economy on every occasion, followed by a higher level
of unemployment as the next step.

JAMES CALLAGHAN, Prime Minister,
Labour Party Conference, 1976

If the Marshall Plan was responsible for facilitating the post-war
economic development in Europe, it had also created the material
conditions for future competitors of the u.s. economy. The
dominance of the dollar was initially challenged by France,
which in 1958 opted for a 'literal translation' of the Bretton
Woods Agreement and began converting its existing dollar
reserves into gold, while promising to do the same with future
dollar inflows. Germany, whose economy and stability was still
too dependent on the u.s., at first refused to follow France down
this path. However, the increased competitiveness of German
exports and the gradual transformation of the u.s. from a trade-
surplus to a trade-deficit economy (with the u.s. importing more
than it was exporting) forced a rethink of the status quo. The

ability of the U.S. to pay foreign debts in its own currency (thus giving them ample monetary freedom), while leaving holders of foreign reserves to deal with the consequences of adjusting their economies to U.S. monetary policy (for example, importing inflation) was incompatible with the type of monetary control that German financial authorities had in mind. The vision of creating a framework of similar exchange rate stability, while disassociating it from the dollar, laid the groundwork for the creation of the European Monetary Union (EMU). But before this became a reality, some other significant changes had taken place.

Keynesianism was essentially a model for social equilibrium designed to stabilize the economy and to manage the threat of social disorder produced by the combined forces of the capitalist crisis of 1929 and the Nazi and Soviet examples. Its predominance after the Second World War rested on balancing the interests of private capital and proletarian needs, while expanding the role and scope of the government through infrastructural projects, public works and (eventually) welfare. By the 1970s, however, the continuation of this balancing act was directly threatening capital profitability. A decline in profitability had also increased pressure towards the opening up of financial opportunities, a condition that necessitated the dismantling of the banking and global capital out- and in-flow regulations. Implementing these necessities was a task taken over by what has since come to be called 'neoliberalism'.[1] Regardless of the accuracy of the term, it is undeniable that a paradigm shift affecting social, legal, economic and political relations took place towards the end of the 1970s, such as the gradual predominance of monetarist economic policies;[2] the transformation of the role of central banks and the increased deregulation of financial institutions; the abandonment of the integrative attitude towards trade unions and workers' demands; the shift away from the public sector through the glorification of the private sector; and, finally, a renewed expansion of capitalist globalization.

Faced with stagflation (the coexistence of inflation and unemployment), Keynesian economists found themselves at a loss, seeing as their calculations could not explain such a development.[3] At first the phenomenon was denied in various ways: inflation was coined as 'exogenous' (as a consequence, for example, of the oil crisis) and temporary, while unemployment was seen as an equally temporary result of falling demand – itself explained by reference to theories of optimum demand (the idea that demand could not rise much more). At the end of the day, however, having failed to understand the persistence of stagflation, it was no wonder that Keynesians could conceive of no policies to combat it. Preoccupied with eliminating waste (in the Keynesian worldview unemployed labour is waste par excellence), the response to falling demand and unemployment included the nationalization of (non-profitable) industries, in the hope that expanding the circulation of money (wages) would generate more demand and rebalance the economy. None of these remedies had any effect.

The monetarists' response was simple: blaming the continuing stagflation on the mistaken insistence of the government to subsidize dying industries and non-productive sectors, they pointed out that increasing the money supply (through deficit spending, nationalizations and job creation) while there was no increase in the production of commodities could only result in inflation. Correctly identifying the oil crisis as only a temporary blip and the diminishing of profits as the real and permanent problem, monetarists sought to reconfigure economic thinking and policy by prioritizing, above all other considerations, a return of profitability at any social cost.

In policy terms, the advent of the monetarist/neoliberal shift can be traced in the unorthodox (at the time) decision of the chairman of the U.S. Federal Reserve, Paul Volcker, in October 1979 to raise U.S. interest rates. Due to the centrality of the U.S. economy and the dollar hegemony within the global capitalist order, the consequences were immediately felt around the world.[4] For Volcker, the primary aim was to contain soaring inflation by reducing the money supply.[5] At an international level, the rationale was to maintain dollar hegemony in an environment where the U.S. (now a deficit country) was losing its ability to exert influence by distributing its surplus abroad (as it had done, for example, through the Marshall Plan). By raising interest rates, the U.S. was thus trying to attract the surpluses of 'competitors' back to the U.S., while retaining the key position of the dollar in international trade.

There was, however, a downside. Domestic investment was slowed down,[6] something that affected the labour market by increasing unemployment and undermining domestic manufacturing industries, plunging the U.S. economy into recession. As a consequence, unemployment figures rose even more, something that was reflected in declining demand. In the monetarist vision, the race against inflation was on and it justified everything: thus while corporate taxes and welfare benefits were slashed, Milton Friedman urged businesses to lay off more workers, 'before inflation does it for you'.

Thanks to the recession, Volcker's 'disinflationary policies' – that is, reduced liquidity and the subsequent recession – were successful in bringing down inflation. At the same time, seeing that unemployment was sharply increasing, the decision was made to 'naturalize' it instead of reducing it: a mere increase of the percentage considered as its 'natural rate' appeared enough.[7] In order to deal with those stubborn workers who did not think so highly of the new monetarist doctors and their prescriptions, a short-sharp-shock remedy was at hand: strikes were met by immediate and relentless repression,[8] a response ideologically justified through an idea that would gain even more ground across the world in the years to come – that of an overvalued and overprotected working class. By creating useful divisions between the perpetually fluid categories of a 'workers' aristocracy' and the 'average worker', bureaucrats, economists and the mass media did their best to present the new dogma as synonymous with rationality and progress, while their enemies were, obviously, backward defenders of a failed system.

The new orthodoxy was not only facilitated by Keynesian inadequacy and the relentless promotion (through, among other means, Nobel Prizes) of the 'soundness' of its economic plans. It also built its strength by breaking and rolling back the previous wave of class antagonism in such an effective way that, only a few years down the line (and possibly ever since), one would be hard pressed to recognize its high-water mark. The foundations for the embrace and nurturing of a culture of narcissistic individualism and an arrogant indifference towards non-commodified relations were significantly strengthened in precisely those times.

The veritable symbol of the onset of what came to be identified as neoliberalism was Ronald Reagan's election as u.s. president in 1981. Almost a year earlier, Margaret Thatcher was elected across the Atlantic on a mandate for ending the 'winter of discontent' that had plagued the UK as a result of its own experience of stagflation and economic slowdown. Following the u.s. example, Thatcher's Conservative government indulged heavily in monetarist trickery: the Medium Term Financial Strategy of 1980 was nothing but a UK version of reducing the money supply (by raising interest rates) in order to control inflation. Immersed in the belief that government actions were at the centre of the failed policies of the past, Thatcher began a sweeping process of privatization and a drastic reduction of the public sector,[9] serving multiple fronts: weakening workers' and trade union bargaining power, reducing the cost of public sector borrowing requirements (and thus deficits) and reversing the policy of the previous Labour government of nationalizing declining or bankrupt industries, such as steel, shipbuilding or aerospace. Finally, as Reagan had, Thatcher reduced welfare, housing and education spending.

Responding to the pressures of the recession that followed, however, the newly acquired orthodoxy of reducing the public sector was partially abandoned. But there was a catch: u.s. government spending was now channelled primarily towards the arms race with the ussr and military budgets, away from any aim of full employment or welfare. In fact, Reagan attempted to offset the increase of spending on the military with more cuts in welfare, education and health. A further relaxation of relevant regulations also facilitated a housing market boom and rising share prices, which, contrary to commodity prices, are not considered as contributing to inflation.[10] A small 'miracle' had taken place: through a mere twist of perspective, deficit spending could continue to rise without any recorded inflation increase.

Just like Keynesian policies adopted in the 1930s, the monetarist promise of growth (read: renewed profits) through inflation control and reduced money supply did not deliver that well. Cutting wages, imposing precarious work relations and destroying unions might be a Pavlovian response to a crisis of profitability but they are not, in themselves, enough to ensure higher returns – especially in the long term.[11] Nor were tax gifts to the rich capable of reversing the profitability decline. These policies were surely successful in reconfiguring class relations and undermining the ability of the labour movement to take advantage of its structural power, but they did little to solve the main problems that the crisis of the 1970s had created. In fact, Reagan's special form of 'military Keynesianism', and Thatcher's monetarist dogmas, only reversed the ongoing recession much later and by taking advantage of another transformation.

## Here Comes Finance

The eventual collapse of the Bretton Woods Agreement in 1971, and the oil crisis of the early 1970s, had accelerated the process of an increased internationalization of the banking sector and financial services, which had been kept in 'check' by the (Keynesian) New Deal response to the 1929 crash. The reversal to a system of managed but floating exchange rates had given breathing space to those who were eager to speculate on the day-to-day fluctuations of currencies and international trade, while also creating financial products that would be advertised as lucrative alternatives to falling profit rates. The monetarist shift thus proved crucial to ingraining the notion that, from here on, economic growth could rely on the expansion of the financial sector,[12] and its ability to simulate significant profits.[13] For this expansion to take place, deregulation was crucial.

At the beginning, the deregulation process was domestic. The u.s. had already abolished Federal requirements on the level of interest rates charged by savings banks in the mid-1970s, freeing them from constraints and promoting engagement in riskier and thus more profitable businesses. When Reagan was elected, the process was formalized and accelerated.[14] At the same time, it was becoming clear that the credit needs of cutting-edge corporations in the international market could no longer be met through domestic banks.[15] The decline of profitability and demand had already sent manufacturers looking towards developing peripheral economies (in Asia, Latin America, Africa and so on) as potential outlets for the relocation of production in environments with more favourable (for capital) labour conditions. But there were several constraints.

On the one hand, the developing economies had no infra-structure capable of accommodating the production and export needs of major manufacturers. On the other, production investments of that scale drained the already limited dollar

reserves of local governments.[16] With the international
expansion of the operations of banks and financial institutions
this predicament changed. Both state-funded infrastructural
and private capital productive investments were now financed
through the expanded and internationalized banking sector,
which, being predominantly dollar-denominated, had high-
interest-bearing loans.[17]

These transformations did more than change the shape of
the global capitalist economy. They also produced new problems
related to the increase of public debt and the foundation of
economic growth on the expansion of credit. But the framework
within which they operated also dictated the type of 'solutions'
these problems would generate: for example, when in 1987 a fight
over interest rates between the u.s. and West Germany caused a
stock exchange crash in the u.s., sending the Dow Jones Industrial
Average (DJIA) down by 22.6 per cent in one day, the newly installed
Federal Reserve chairman, Alan Greenspan, created $12 billion of
new bank reserves by buying up government securities. The $12
billion injection caused the Fed Funds rate to fall by three-quarters
of a point, but it did halt the financial panic. This sent a crucial
and historic message around that the Central Bank was officially
acquiring the role of 'lender of last resort', in other words, that
central banks were more than willing to print money in order to
bail out financial and banking crises.

This could have been the first opportunity to foresee that
there was something fundamentally unstable about an economy
that measures its growth on credit expansion, while assigning
the authorities the role of taking responsibility for its negative
consequences. But the orthodoxy of the time forbade such
thoughts. Instead, the UK went through a similar transformation,
which started in 1979 with the abolition of exchange controls and
reached its peak with the 'Big Bang' reforms of 1986. In the same
year, the EU tried to keep up by signing the Single European Act,
which, apart from enhancing a single market for commodities and

services, abolished capital controls and other restrictions on finance. By the end of the 1980s most major capitalist countries had lifted most forms of capital control.

## Singles and Markets

Faced with free-floating exchange rates after the collapse of Bretton Woods, the initial response of European countries was to establish a system of relatively fixed exchange rates.[18] But the attempt to mimic the structure of the dollar hegemony and use the most stable currency (the West Deutsch Mark) as a yardstick for all other European currencies failed, as it forced all other economies to follow closely Germany's monetary policy of regularly raising interest rates. The UK abandoned it only two months after joining and France followed suit two years later, in 1974.

While this experience put a halt to discussions for further monetary union, the need for exchange rate stability was persistent. As such, another attempt was made in 1979, when the French president Giscard d'Estaing and the German chancellor Helmut Schmidt introduced the European Monetary System (EMS). The EMS, a major component of which was the Exchange Rate Mechanism (ERM), was a system of so-called 'semi-pegged' currencies which established an overall margin within which currency fluctuations could be accepted, with some currencies (the Italian lira, the Spanish peseta, the Portuguese escudo and the UK sterling) allowed wider fluctuations than others. Quite importantly it also included, at the request of Germany, a clause that called for rigorous control of the inflation rate.

With the global economy still recovering from Volcker's shock and monetarist orthodoxy making its baby steps in the governments of Reagan and Thatcher, François Mitterrand was elected in France on a Keynesian mandate of anti-austerity and a mission to combat recession. Contrary to the previous governments' decision to keep a stable franc while sacrificing jobs and economic activity, Mitterrand opted for an approach premised on deficit spending, job creation and lower interest rates. Riding a populist wave, he also blamed the economic slowdown on 'speculative finance'. Mitterrand was referring to the fact that the continuing global recession had allowed speculators to undermine the French economy by betting that the franc would again be forced to devaluate. Increased speculation led to a massive capital flight that drove up borrowing costs and spiked inflation. Desperate, and illustrating once again the dependence of the French economy, Mitterrand asked West Germany for help. Germany agreed but, in a move that would be repeated forty years later with Greece, only in exchange for a programme that curtailed inflation and imposed a wage freeze and significant cuts in public spending. After an initial period during which Mitterrand seriously considered abandoning the EMS and free floating the franc, he eventually conceded.[19]

The austerity programme that Jacques Delors masterminded and Mitterrand implemented was meant to counteract the 'catastrophic deficit' in the inter-trade with Germany and France's domestic economic troubles. Using the excuse of battling against France's potential isolation from the European Community, Mitterrand's Left government embraced monetarist dogma, focusing its economic policy on controlling the money supply and inflation. But this capitulation was not just passive. Giving credence to the notion that the Left is quite often more capable of defending the capitalist economy than the Right, Mitterrand's government actively produced a 'scientific' demonization of deficit spending, in the form of the (ever-since-dominant) dogma that a deficit of more than 3 per cent of GDP is destructive for the economy. The way in which this specific number came about was explained in an article of 2010 by Guy Abeille, one of Mitterrand's economic advisers at the time, and is worth quoting at length:

> One late night [in 1981] I and Rolland de Villepin received a call from Pierre Bilger, no. 2 at the Ministry . . . He informed us in a few words of the budgetary disaster that we were facing, and told us that the president [Mitterrand] himself urgently and personally asked us to come up with a rule, simple and useful, that carries the aura of expertise, a rule to use against all those who wished to devour the budget [i.e. deficit spending]. We had to hurry. Neither Villepin nor I had any idea what to do, as there was no economic theory to help us devise this rule . . .
>
> We went through public expenditure, its size, its structure, with debt, without debt, its rate of increase in relation to that of the economy. We thought we could come up with something, but . . . nothing. All we got were some weak recommendations, not at all impressive, unsuitable to be used as a spear against the monster of public expenses. We decided to turn it around and look at the issue from the point of view of the taxation rate in relation to national income. But taxes are not a constant variable . . .
>
> The only thing that was left was the public deficit. First of all, the word 'deficit' is commonly understood, from the average citizen to the President himself, this way: we have a deficit, therefore we do not have enough money . . . Moreover, from Keynes onwards, the notion of the public deficit had acquired an honorary role: it is one of the most common terms used in economic theories and one of the most functional variables of economic models. It soon became clear: the public deficit, and only that, had the prestige and the phenomenological clarity that we needed to accomplish what was asked of us . . .

It did not take long to find the best way to use it. For the best recourse for every strapped economist is the Gross Domestic Product (GDP): everything starts and ends with the GDP; all the bulky figures are measured in relation to the GDP. Therefore: the simple, useful but also 'scientific' rule that they were asking from us was the deficit/GDP ratio.

All that was left was to find a ratio. It did not take us more than 2 seconds. We looked at the latest GDP projection. We added the ghost of the 100 billion franc deficit that was looming over our desk. We divided the one by the other and came up with 3 per cent.

We did have some afterthoughts, to be honest . . . The public deficit is nothing but debt: it is a specific amount of money that you need to borrow, which means you have to ask someone to lend money to you, and then you have to save that money in the next years to pay it back. In other words, to determine a ratio of deficit to GDP, we have to compare a money flow, divided into maturing debts that have to be repaid in the following years, with the wealth that has been produced in the year in which the debt was made. There is an obvious temporal discontinuity . . . To focus on the deficit of a given year has no meaning whatsoever, and it is even more absurd to compare it with the GDP of the same year. The deficit/GDP ratio can thus only act as an indication, that gives us a vague impression of the situation, but it cannot, in any case, be used as a compass, as it measures absolutely nothing.[20]

As monetarism came to dominate economic policy-making in the majority of European countries, discussions on the necessity of a monetary union accelerated on a new grounding. Indicatively, the signing of the Single European Act of 1986–7 eliminated trade barriers, while also further removing restrictions on finance and banking for EU members.[21] It also called for the creation of a single, free-trade market for the whole of the EU by 1992. Two years later,

France and Germany would jointly announce that a European
monetary union could well be a reality within the next ten years.

## Maastricht Gridlock

In 1991, only a few months after the collapse of the Soviet
Union and with German unification still a source of instability,[22]
European politicians signed the Maastricht Treaty. Its significance is not merely historical: the Treaty not only represented
a flavoured distillation of a decade of monetarist ingredients,
but spelled out the rules that have determined, to a very large
extent, the response to the Eurozone crisis of 2010. In brief,
the Maastricht Treaty urged the independence of all member-
state central banks, while seeking inflation, interest and
exchange rate convergence. Most importantly, it demanded
a tightening of fiscal belts, setting out clear targets: budget
deficits limited by the magical 3 per cent and public debt at
60 per cent of GDP. It also outlined the steps for the creation
of the EMU's own central bank, the European Central Bank
(ECB), charged with overseeing the proper functioning of
the common policies and currency.

The institutional structure of the ECB formalized both
its independence and its powers to pursue the Maastricht
criteria. In this way, it reflected an architectural design that
would prove key to the structure of the whole Eurozone: the
Maastricht Treaty prohibited any external interference with
the ECB while refraining from placing any reciprocal restrictions
on the ECB's ability to impose economic policy. This structure
essentially and eventually meant that the ECB's primary aims
(with price stability – that is, inflation control – at the very top
of the list) could not be changed institutionally, while at the same
time national governments would be (and were) consistently and
unreservedly pushed into reconfiguring their labour, commodities,
services and credit markets along monetarist lines.

It was quite clear that the convergence criteria for joining the monetary union were primarily designed to accomodate the needs (and fears) of the German economy.[23] In this context, the Treaty also included a clause against any bail-out mechanism for weak-performing economies, as well as prohibiting the direct financing of deficit by the ECB. This clause was quite crucial (and it would prove very crucial in the future Eurocrisis too), as it responded to fears within Germany and other northern European countries that a common currency would result in a certain surplus recycling mechanism that would hand over Germany's surplus to fiscally undisciplined countries of the South.[24] Given that support for the common currency project in Germany was very low at the time, Chancellor Kohl was continually forced to repeat the existence of this clause at every Bundestag meeting to discuss the Maastricht Treaty.

## Keep your Friends Close and your Enemies Closer

The only request of Germany that was not met at the time concerned the limitation of EMU participation to a small number of northwestern European countries (Germany, France and Benelux). Instead, the invitation was extended to Ireland, Austria, Denmark, Finland and – adding to Germany's nervousness – to Spain, Portugal and Italy (Greece was not even considered in these early discussions). With the Maastricht criteria as the yardstick, these concerns made sense: most potential member states (and especially the Southern ones) had deficit/debt figures way off the required ones. But the outbreak of the exchange rate wars of the early 1990s inadvertently indicated how this gridlock was to be overcome.

The German reunification of 1990 had caused domestic inflation to rise to 4 per cent, something relatively normal for other European countries but absolute anathema for inflation-phobic Germany. Horrified by this, the Bundesbank immediately sought to counteract it by raising interest rates. At the time, however, most European national currencies (even the British pound) were pegged to each other through the European Exchange Rate Mechanism (ERM), thus forced to follow the strongest currency (the Deutsch Mark). When Germany raised its interest rates to stave off its inflationary pressures, the rest were compelled to follow suit.

But the policy of raising interest rates (as Germany was continually doing) could not be followed ad infinitum by other countries, especially once the recessionary effects of conforming to the Maastricht convergence criteria were hitting them.[25] Moreover, raising interest rates in some countries, such as Italy, meant adding percentage points to their already increased deficits, moving even farther away from the convergence targets. The common cause of European integration had already taken a serious hit from the refusal of Denmark to sign the Maastricht Treaty (June 1992), and a possible repeat of such a result in France's own upcoming referendum (in September 1992) was threatening to derail all hopes of monetary union. Faced with these developments, ERM members urged Germany, in the summer of 1992, to cut interest rates and give them some breathing space. Preoccupied with its own problems and ideological obsessions, Germany refused.

As currency speculators felt that the possibility of the ERM crumbling was looming, they started targeting currency after currency, forcing both massive reserves spending and devaluations. Italy devalued the lira by 7 per cent, while the Bank of France was forced to spend more than 32 billion dollars from its reserves to keep the franc from plummeting. (Coincidentally, of course, the Bundesbank's reserves rose by 40 billion in the same period.) The UK tried in vain to raise interest rates, twice on the same day, only to be forced to take the pound entirely out of the ERM.

The currency depreciations that ensued drove budget deficits further up, mirroring an increase in social security spending and lowering of taxation to counteract the recession. This meant that most countries were once again moving away from the Maastricht targets, casting further doubt on the prospect of monetary union, especially since Germany stubbornly translated these developments as indications of a lack of fiscal discipline. But the erupting panic offered another insight, one perfectly summarized by a member of the Bundesbank Council:

> I would not previously have forecast that the European Currency would start during the 1990s. The decisive moment came with the currency crisis of 1992–1993. The status quo was not tenable. We faced a 30 per cent devaluation of the lire. Some companies in Southern Germany competing with Italy went bankrupt. There was a danger of controls on movement and goods. I and others came to the conclusion that the Common Market would not survive another crisis of this dimension.[26]

Far from the disguised fear that the 'Common Market' could not withstand another such episode of turbulence, the importance of the above passage lies in the admission that the main reason for accepting countries with high inflation, off-target budget deficits and debts (such as Italy[27]) in the monetary union was precisely in order to reduce the threat from their weapon par excellence against foreign competition: currency devaluation.[28] This simple fact lay behind the decision to change course and allow EMU participation for countries that showed 'progress towards' convergence criteria, rather than their achievement.[29] And it also explains the essence behind future complaints regarding the loss of national sovereignty that EMU participation entailed.

    In an ironic twist, a combination of the above events would eventually be utilized to convince the populations of Southern countries also to abandon the ability to control monetary policy. On the one hand, the fiscal belt-tightening that was part of the convergence process had reduced inflation, budget deficits, unit labour costs and similar monetarist targets. At the same time, the repeated currency devaluations across Europe had assisted competitiveness. By pointing simultaneously at both these developments (without pointing at the fact that the second one would be lost as soon as the EMU would come to life), pro-monetary union voices would claim that the difficult adjustment process was already bearing fruit, and growth was already a reality. The renewed confidence in the EMU project generated by such numbers and exclamations was successful in mystifying the structural imbalance that was being produced. More importantly, the convergence of interest rates towards the German ones already meant that (especially Southern) European countries suddenly enjoyed lower debt-servicing costs, allowing the expansion of credit and thus hiding declining real wages, while providing a generous hint as to what membership in the Eurozone would be like. If there were any doubts left about the EMU, they were ignored. The choice of the day was the conscious decision to follow the path explained by Bundesbank President Hans Tietmeyer during the opening of the ECB headquarters in Frankfurt in 1998:

> Monetary union means a restriction on national sovereignty, on national manoeuvring room and the ability to go it alone. Participants lose the instrument of exchange rate adjustments. That strengthens pressures towards internal flexibility. In a monetary union, countries have to tackle and solve their economic problems and challenges in a similar way and with similar speed. If the countries decide fundamentally different answers, then great problems will arise. Countries which implement the right solutions soon become more competitive against those who react wrongly or late.[30]

*three*

# A Green Sun

PASOK was created by Andreas Papandreou, the son of Georgios Papandreou, an eminent figure in Greek politics since the end of the Second World War.[1] Andreas had started his political career under the wing of his father,[2] but his rise to prominence came after his anti-dictatorship organization, the Panhellenic Liberation Movement (PAK), was transformed into the Panhellenic Socialist Movement (PASOK) a few months after the collapse of the junta in 1974. PASOK borrowed many of the organizational structures of a Left that seemed unable to mobilize significant support,[3] although post-dictatorship social and political conditions could be regarded as particularly favourable. Centred around a charismatic leader and a strictly hierarchical anatomy, reminiscent of the 'democratic centralism' of Leninist parties, the development of PASOK into a mass party was premised on its left-leaning yet ambiguous language, and the party's cross-section unifying element and main appeal was an inclusive social-democratic programme *and* the reappropriation of patriotism from the right wing's historical monopoly.[4] Early alliances with the centrist and widely recognized anti-dictatorial 'Democratic Defence' organization allowed PASOK to expand its anti-junta credentials, providing an opportunity to bridge centrist/democratic forces with a left-leaning language much more popular at the time. For the first time in Greece's history, the Left was given the chance to participate in economic development – or, in any case, in discussions about it.

Commentators and political analysts of different convictions have repeated and condemned the 'populist' character of PASOK, either stressing its 'betrayal' of left principles or its opportunistic usage of them to consolidate its power-mongering. Though populism is certainly an undeniable feature of its historical trajectory, the monotony of the accusation misinterprets the historical material conditions that led to PASOK's dominance. Keeping a safe distance from the (more or less) pro-Soviet Left, PASOK promised a Keynesian road to growth that appealed to a very large segment of the population that had been, politically and economically, effectively marginalized by decades of right-wing hegemony and clientelism. This inclusive economic outlook included progressive transformations at the social level too – such as formal women's equality and the legitimation of political marriage, to name some key examples – transformations that torpedoed traditional right-wing institutions such as the family or the Church. But in doing so, PASOK was not only expressing a range of demands coming from below, it was ventriloquizing the needs of a restructuring process of private capital, whose modernizing interests could no longer be carried through by the anachronistic police state of the Right.

## The Early Years

We have seen how the government of Karamanlis attempted to revive the economy after its exposure to the international crisis of the 1970s through the adoption of Keynesian-styled policies, along with a certain relaxation of political repression. The necessity of such a strategy, however, had generated a double problematic: on the one hand, a mass wave of wildcat strikes had forced significant wage increases, seriously exceeding productivity output. On the other hand, the combined result of strike insurgency and exposure to the international crisis had convinced private capital to move away from direct investments (primarily in manufacture) and seek engagement in other sectors of the economy (predominantly, the tertiary sector) deemed more profitable and less exposed to international competition. The consequence was explosive: the demonstrated inability of the Right both to control social antagonism and to accommodate the needs of both large sections of the population and private capital paved the way for PASOK.

When PASOK came to power in 1981, eleven out of nineteen industrial sectors of Greece were already recording losses. Loyal to the Keynesian model of regarding all utilization of labour as the way out of an economic slowdown, PASOK proceeded with bail-outs and subsidies for an important number of these sectors. To facilitate this, PASOK made important changes in the structure of the Bank of Greece and its fiscal policy, while creating the necessary institutional forms that would manage the state loans to support private or nationalized capital.[5] In the context of promoting Greece's economic ability to sustain itself independently, it also heralded an ambitious programme of redirecting the manufacturing sector into heavier industry, with PASOK's ministers announcing the creation of state-led coal, steel and nickel industries. In line with the Keynesian approach of prioritizing demand, PASOK introduced the mechanism of Automatic Inflation Adjustment (ATA), which implemented wage increases on the basis of predicted future inflation. Hoping that these changes would accelerate GDP growth rates, PASOK relied heavily on deficit spending.

Papandreou's pre-election promise to boost the job market, increase wages and end the political marginalization of large sections of the working class occurred through an economic policy whose goal was to increase the quantity of money in circulation, to allow moderate inflation (with its redistribution of wealth) and to reduce unemployment through (primarily) state sector employment schemes. But PASOK was also particularly interested in containing the militancy of the working class, a goal that necessitated the reconfiguration of trade union politics. In this context, PASOK declared war on the 'complacent, right wing-led and pro-employer' trade unions of the time (a more or less accurate description) and proclaimed their transformation into a 'class-oriented, politically motivated trade union movement, independent from the state, employers and parties'.[6] The rhetoric was, however, rather misleading. The aim was to dismantle the right-wing stranglehold over these institutions and to replace it with PASOK hegemony. When that was not possible, PASOK proceeded to abolish existing structures and create new ones (as happened with many managerial councils or small company committees).

The trade union sector did not share this fate alone. In fact, a veritable 'march through the institutions' at virtually all levels of the state apparatus took place in the early years of PASOK's rule, creating the conditions under which, only a few years later, it would be quite difficult to differentiate between PASOK as political party and PASOK as state mechanism. Nonetheless, contrary to contemporary (and mostly neoliberal) accounts, this predicament was by no means a PASOK novelty. Even if one leaves aside the historical foundations of such phenomena that date from the creation of the modern Greek state,[7] right-wing rule was based on identical principles. If there was something worth noting in relation to PASOK's management of this age-old tradition, it was the fact that, for the first time in the post-war period, the government did not systematically repress and marginalize those that it did not accommodate. In conjunction with the expansionary economic policy pursued by Papandreou, the resulting economic growth and inequality reduction convinced a significant majority of the population to fall in line behind PASOK.

This did not come without a price. The end of political marginalization, the public sector jobs for those previously deprived of them, the wage increases that followed inflation – all of these were premised on the acceptance of PASOK's wider vision and developmental programme and the recuperation of workplace struggles. In this context, and as early as 1982, Papandreou called for workers to abandon 'irrational demands'[8] (such as further increases in wages) and focus instead on how better to attract investments, increase productivity and conform to the new production norms.[9] The necessity to exert control over class antagonisms, especially in the public sector, even led Papandreou essentially to outlaw public sector strikes,[10] while the complaints of representatives of private capital at the time that PASOK's policies disproportionately favoured workers was further contradicted by the expansion of precarious and temporary work.[11]

As a serious Keynesian, Papandreou had no interest in antagonizing the private capital sector. Rather, he was concerned about its anaemic performance and its 'refusal' to commit to increasing investments. He thus sought to create the best conditions for this to take place, confessing that 'private [capital] initiative is our priority for economic recovery'. But he quickly added that if the private sector did not take advantage of the support and opportunities offered from PASOK, this priority 'will be replaced by the Banks and public investments'.[12]

It is through this prism that the troubled relationship between PASOK and private capital, often represented by the Union of Greek Industrialists (SEB), can best be examined. On the one hand, PASOK wished to engage both labour and capital in a development programme with increased competitiveness and rising productivity as its stated goals, with workers benefiting through its expansionary economic policy with rising wages as an exchange. The other side of this strategy, however, required private capital to fulfil its part of the bargain, that is, increase productive investments. Faced with reduced competitiveness (directly related to EU membership and the effects of the international crisis[13]), the change of focus towards the tertiary sector and domestic profit margin losses, due to the effects of the previous period's proletarian struggles, private capital failed to comply. At the economic level, the situation was becoming explosive.

## A 'Neoliberal' Love Affair

Four years after its triumphant election, PASOK faced an economic situation of minimal (private or foreign direct) investment and declining industrial profits, accompanied by repeated state bailouts and nationalizations that put pressure on state deficit figures. At the same time, public sector wages continued to be automatically adjusted (thanks to ATA) to an inflation rate that had reached 25 per cent, while productivity rates in all sectors remained below wages. The possibility that renewed growth would allow (in typical Keynesian fashion) for an increase in taxation that would compensate for state spending was further undermined by PASOK's political choice not to antagonize private capital and increase corporate taxation further.

In the context of these developments, PASOK started to 'rethink' its direction. The 1983 state budget had already included a number of wage freezes on certain sectors, along with more capital tax exemptions (especially for multinational corporations), albeit unsuccessfully. Similar frail attempts were made in 1984, but the overwhelming desire to win the coming elections of 1985 meant that PASOK was still willing to allow the economy to slow down (and wages to go up) rather than implement unpopular measures. As soon as PASOK won the 1985 parliamentary elections (with a slightly decreased percentage in relation to 1981), however, economic recovery was placed at the top of the agenda. And 'economic recovery', according to the doctrine of the day, meant wage cuts and austerity. Papandreou handed over the task of implementing this difficult change in strategy to the new Finance Minister, Kostas Simitis.

Simitis's project (the so-called 'Stabilization Programme') could well have been copied and pasted from some neoliberal textbook of the period, blaming high production costs (that is, wages) as responsible for reduced productivity, and competitiveness.[14] Reduced competitiveness meant reduced exports and thus an indication of a deficit in the current account balance. The Yearly Report of the Bank of Greece set the tone:[15] since a deficit current account balance was the main obstacle to a viable economic policy, the government was forced to effect a 'radical shift in its economic policies'.[16] First and foremost, this government had to abandon the macroeconomic (Keynesian) model and join the contemporaneous chorus against inflationary pressures. According to the same report, the Keynesian model had failed to produce 'the suitable, for today's changing economic developments, type of businessman',[17] something that explained the anaemic performance of the private sector during all previous years. The path to follow was clear: inflation control, deficit spending cuts and a wage freeze in order to restore productivity rates and competitiveness.

The measures were wholeheartedly welcomed by the Union of Greek Industrialists, who went so far as proclaiming that 'it is the first time that, after all these years, there is a common perspective [with the government] on the needs of the economy'.[18] The days when government and PASOK-led trade unions blamed private capital for an 'investment strike', while the employers blamed the government for repressing 'private initiative', were gone. Under the guidance of Papandreou, who officially declared the wish to minimize the role of the state in economic affairs,[19] Simitis proceeded with a 15.5 per cent devaluation of the drachma (in order to boost export competitiveness) and a drastic transformation of the ATA mechanism.[20] Along the same lines, Simitis put a stop to public sector hiring and public investment, while promoting the privatization or even shutting down of certain (formerly nationalized) industries and corporations. He also promised to 'rationalize' the tax collection system.

The measures produced dramatic results: inflation was reduced from 25 per cent to 16 per cent in one year, while the government deficit was almost cut in half. At the same time, labour costs in Greece fell by 13 per cent, in contrast to the 16 per cent increase recorded as an EU average at the same time. And although government debt was still on the rise, it remained primarily internal (and thus easier to refinance) and not foreign, another indication of the fact that the state was still both the main employer and the main investor in Greece.[21]

## A Big, Fat State

To an important degree, the ideological form inherent in the 'Stabilization Programme', with its attacks on the conditions of work and reproduction, was grounded on an argument that would continue to characterize public discourse in Greece and which witnessed a timely renewal after the 2010 'sovereign debt' crisis. This was none other than the repetitive claim that the public sector in Greece was 'too enlarged', that it was 'unproductive' and thus a great burden on the state budget. The 1985 shift in economic policy coincided with the first time that Greek workers were chastised for being 'lazy' and 'living above their means', while the notion of full employment was declared nothing but a 'negative residue of the past'. As this depiction has been used consistently by all those who salivate over the term 'economic restructuring', it is worth examining thoroughly.

When complaints about Greece's 'overmanned' public sector came to the surface, PASOK had, in fact, increased public sector employment.[22] However, the percentage of public employees in Greece was lower than in most OECD countries (Greece was in thirteenth place). What did contribute to the budget burden were some increases in welfare expenditures (such as healthcare) and, more importantly, capital tax cuts. It was (and remains) easier to speak abstractly of an enlarged public sector,[23] and therefore of the need to sack workers or else to stop employment trends, than to effect capital tax increases, especially when the private sector is seen as the backbone of a 'healthy' economy and is charged with attracting involvement and investments. In reality, the so-called enlarged public sector was, though slightly larger than in previous years, clearly smaller than the European standard of the time. Yet the strategy of demonizing the public sector and thus facilitating lay-offs was intended to direct more workers towards the private sector, where conditions of work were harder, lower paid and more precarious. In this way, it was thought, public spending could be reduced without any need to increase capital taxation.

A similar argument could be made about government debt. Economic analysts and commentators of the time warned that government debt had an excessive upward trend, primarily as a result of public spending. A quick look at the numbers verifies this assertion, as state debt, both internal and external, rose from 39.7 per cent of GDP in 1981 to 80 per cent in 1989.[24] Again, this was directly connected with public spending, which includes wages but also investment. A closer look at the European context, however, shows that public spending in Greece, even at its peak in 1985, remained below the EU average (48 per cent as against 49.1 per cent). The fundamental difference was that Greek public spending reached that percentage (48 per cent) by increasing, whereas the EU average was a result of decreases. In other words, Greek economic policy was not keeping up to date with the established orthodoxy of spending cuts, wage cuts and welfare cuts.

A third area that came to the surface during the shift of 1985, and which also remained a constant complaint for years to come, was the expansion of the service (tertiary) sector at the expense of the primary (agriculture, fishing, mining) and the secondary (manufacturing) sectors. The argument was that this uneven expansion was responsible for undermining Greece's competitiveness, while destroying its industrial capacity, making it more vulnerable to, and dependent on, foreign credit and/or imports. Again, actual data might help: from 1981 to 1990 the primary sector declined from 14.2 per cent of GDP to 11 per cent, while the secondary dropped from 31.9 per cent to 30.4 per cent. The tertiary sector, however, rose from 53.9 per cent to 58.6 per cent of GDP in the same period. To be precise, it is important to remember that the shift of private capital towards the tertiary sector started before PASOK, reflecting the manner through which the private sector responded to the effects of EU membership, reduced export competitiveness and workers' combativeness. Nonetheless, despite the fact that this trend had been initiated by private capital, PASOK's government proved more than willing to embrace it. This is what lay behind the open endorsement of the expansion of the service sector by the head of the Central Bank of Greece Dimitris Chalikias in 1985, a position justified by claiming that the service sector represented an economic competitive advantage for Greece and a 7.6 per cent contribution to GDP in the course of the previous six years.[25]

## The End of the Affair

This period of austerity continued almost uninterrupted for the next two years, despite worsening conditions for workers, mostly due to the strong popularity of Papandreou. A wave of strikes in 1988 and 1989, however, and the prospect of losing the forthcoming elections, meant that Papandreou became more concerned with retaining his (and PASOK's) popularity than with continuing the 'stabilization' (that is, neoliberal restructuring) process assigned to Simitis. Papandreou thus proceeded to fire Simitis from the Finance Ministry, pretending that the recessionary policies were not his doing and attempting to return to an expansionary fiscal policy.

Naturally, private capital was gravely disappointed by this
U-turn. But PASOK was not particularly happy with the fact that
private capital still refrained from opening up and commencing
investments. In this context, Papandreou proceeded to
materialize what had, since 1986, only been a threat against the
continuing reluctance of private capital to take on the economic
role that Papandreou demanded:

> Gentlemen, you are the industrialist class – I refer to the
> well-known names – you have the opportunity, you have the
> support, but if you do not feel you are up to the task, if you
> are used to living on loans, if this is how things go, then we
> . . . will create a new industrialist class, who will take over
> the new opportunities that are opening up and will build
> a new industry in Greece, one that can survive.[26]

The rapid emergence of this 'new class' of entrepreneurs was met,
however, with strong resistance from the majority of established
capitalists who initiated a systematic deconstruction of their
previous allies, Papandreou, PASOK and the whole state apparatus.
In what became known as the 'dirty 1989', a series of scandals
entered the public domain, most of them 'exposed' by an alliance
of industrialists, businessmen and, quite crucially, media moguls.[27]
One scandal concerned the fact that the state's secret services
had tapped the phones of political opponents of the government,
while another concerned the gross misappropriation of EU funds.
But the most indicative scandal of the time, which would
eventually lead to the collapse of Papandreou's PASOK, was directly
related to the new entrepreneurial class and one of its key
representatives, George Koskotas.

Koskotas was a low-level ex-banker who rose to fame and
power as an example of Papandreou's attempt to replace the
existing business class with people more willing to toe the party
line. Thus, when Koskotas bought a 56 per cent majority share

in the Bank of Crete where he was employed, the government immediately gave him a tremendous boost by transferring all public employee bank accounts (that is, wage payments) to his bank. At the same time, Papandreou's wish to dominate the privately owned media landscape meant that Koskotas ended up as the owner of three newspapers and five popular magazines. In its counter-attack, and claiming that part of the funds with which Koskotas bought the majority of shares in Bank of Crete came from embezzlement along with bribes to top PASOK members, the threatened business class achieved not only the arrest and imprisonment of Koskotas but the near-collapse of the government.

## The Return of the Vampires

Eventually, when the 1989 elections took place, Papandreou's rule came to an end. Shortly before the change of guard, however, PASOK had used its majority position to change the electoral law, thus making it increasingly difficult for a party to form a majority government. As a result, though PASOK lost the elections, the opposition New Democracy (ND) party failed to form a government. Jumping on the bandwagon with an air of moral superiority and the desire to see an end to their sidelining by PASOK, the newly formed coalition of the KKE and KKE ES (who had joined forces and formed the party of 'Synaspismos' in 1989, a development heavily influenced by the collapse of the USSR) answered the call for a 'cleansing' of the political landscape and agreed to participate in an interim government whose 'sole' purpose would be to overcome the gridlock in a judicial manner and take those responsible to court.

While the climate was being prepared for the settling of scores with PASOK on a legal level, the ND-led government (with the support of Left deputies and ministers) tried to fill in the governmental gap and consolidate itself through generous handouts, such as tax amnesties to big debtors or the flushing of municipalities with plenty of money. To deal with the slowdown in the economy, which some have claimed was close to defaulting, the state issued short-term bonds at incredible rates (by the end of 1989 the rate had reached 27 per cent!). This allowed the government some breathing space but also increased the deficit by a staggering 13 per cent of GDP. No matter how hard the head of the Bank of Greece, Dimitrios Chalikias, tried to convince the government to reinstate the rudely interrupted 'Stabilization Programme' of Simitis,[28] it soon became clear that New Democracy had a slightly different version of neoliberalism in mind.

Strengthened by a second election round, which provided them with a slight majority, New Democracy embarked on a frenzy of privatizations for which they tried to get wider support by calling them 'de-nationalizations'. These included the sale of all enterprises that belonged to state banks, the liberalization of the energy and telecommunications sector, and the privatization of the railroad and air travel. New Democracy's finance minister, Giorgos Souflias, took his job very seriously: he attempted to change the pension system and to widen the tax base, while introducing new tax criteria for the self-employed. Moreover, he added a surplus tax in the housing market, increased VAT by 2 per cent, withdrew a series of tax gifts, abolished ATA altogether, institutionalized part-time work and, finally, imposed longer opening hours for shops. As if this was not enough, a wide-ranging restructuring of the education system was added to the mix. Unbeknownst to the government, they had very quickly reached the end of the line.

The struggles that erupted around education and the privatization of public transport shook the government to its core. The situation produced bitter memories of the right-wing's repressive past and its widespread use of police violence to suppress dissent, especially in relation to education reform. New Democracy did, of course, blame PASOK and its grip on trade unions for the mobilizations – an accusation with a certain element of truth – but this could not divert attention from the fact that a teacher was murdered by thugs belonging to the youth organization of New Democracy or that the police's heavy-handed response during extensive riots in the centre of Athens in January 1991 resulted in the deaths of four people.[29] The climate produced by these events, as well as the widespread attacks on living conditions from the neoliberal reforms, took its toll on the government.

If the internal antagonisms were not enough, the u.s. invasion of Iraq and the outbreak of the Gulf War only accelerated the government's slide, as the already weak economic performance took another hit due to the hike in oil prices. And as for the last stand of the government, their cherished privatizations, these were officially ended in 1992 after Finance Minister Giannis Palaiokrasas announced the willingness of the government to sell 35 Aegean islands, causing outrage and rendering the whole process ridiculous.

Caught in its own national myths, New Democracy sought to overcome all its problems by seeking refuge in diehard nationalism, whose main target became the attempt to deny neighbouring Macedonia the use of the name Macedonia. In the sorry debacle that followed, and although Mitsotakis tried to minimize the extent of international humiliation by changing course, causing the resignation of Antonis Samaras (then foreign minister), the damage was already done. Soon after, New Democracy lost its parliamentary majority and was forced into another round of elections.

The short-lived government of New Democracy had managed to make the economy even worse in only a few years. The wish to increase state income through privatizations had failed miserably,[30] while the social struggles that had emerged against the majority of proposed reforms had brought Greece to the brink of explosion, derailing any hopes of viable economic restructuring. The 1994 Yearly Report of the Bank of Greece summed up the array of failures in rather harsh language:

> The economic developments in 1993 are predominantly characterised by the discrepancy of the basic elements of the Greek economy from the targets that were set or even the predictions that were made in the beginning of the year, especially in relation to public deficit and debt, the diffusion of inflation and the rate of economic growth.[31]

In this short period, New Democracy had exhibited its complete inability to take advantage of PASOK's collapse. At a time of worldwide neoliberal ascendancy, due to the collapse of the USSR and its satellites, and the ideological hegemony of the free market, New Democracy tried to implement its vision of neoliberal reforms while retaining the state as the fundamental mediator,[32] and simultaneously obsessively aligning itself with the most reactionary elements of Greek society, such as rampant nationalism and the anachronism of the scandalously wealthy Church. Any attempt to exploit the economic opportunities opened up by the breaking up of ex-socialist Balkan countries (through both significant investments in those countries and the savage exploitation of the migrants that came to Greece as a result of economic and social collapse) was somehow internally sabotaged and over-shadowed by reactionary nationalism, which often led Greece to align itself with strange bedfellows, such as the Serbian butcher Slobodan Milošević.[33]

In a last effort to win the following elections, the government indulged in another pre-election spending spree (more than 325 billion drachmas above predictions, as the Yearly Report of the Bank of Greece claimed), thus succeeding in bringing the debt/GDP ratio to a staggering 111.6 per cent, an almost 30 per cent increase in one year.[34] But the near-complete loss of legitimacy meant that when

New Democracy lost the following elections, no one was particularly surprised.[35] Andreas Papandreou won the elections of 1993, but his frail health dominated this period, whose only noteworthy events concern the consolidation of the strategy for meeting the Maastricht criteria and a conflict with Turkey over a small rock in the Aegean, which almost led the two countries to war. Andreas Papandreou resigned as prime minister in January 1996 and died later that year. He was replaced by Kostas Simitis, who set out to 'complete' his 1986 'stabilization programme', this time with the added aim of bringing Greece to a convergence path with the rest of the EU in accordance with the criteria for joining the Eurozone club.

## Darling, Let's Get Modernized[36]

Even today, the term 'PASOK' is inextricably linked to Andreas Papandreou, as the changes effected in Greek society during his rule signified a rupture with the country's past and achieved a unification and integration of a large part of the Greek population that had been marginalized by the policies of the Right. Coupled with the lasting effects of the expansionary policies of the early years and of the reconfiguration of the state mechanism as the executive apparatus of PASOK's vision, the symbolic power of the image of Andreas Papandreou persisted long after his political and physical demise. In reality, however, PASOK ruled over Greece under the leadership of Kostas Simitis for a longer period.[37] Importantly, Simitis governed Greece while it prepared for EMU membership, a period that laid the foundations for both the performance of the Greek economy as a Eurozone member and, crucially, its eventual economic collapse in 2010.

The Stabilization Programme of 1985 was the first time that Simitis put his ideas into practice. Adopting the monetarist targets of the period (anti-inflation, reducing current account deficits and boosting export competitiveness), the new direction was described as the only way to improve declining profitability, facilitate investment from the private sector and support an industrial sector that had been in decline. And though Papandreou officially terminated the Stabilization Programme in 1987, its effect in reorienting the general economic outlook was long-standing. In the period between 1987 and 1994, all the indicators of capital accumulation in Greece were transformed: labour costs were reduced, profitability was increased, and the replacement of labour by constant capital was also accelerated, steadily increasing the unemployment rate in a novel 'naturalized' form.

At its initial phase, indicating its macroeconomic vision, and contrary to the official position held by private capital (as expressed by SEB) that the problem of profitability was reducible to increasing wages, a close associate of Simitis, Tasos Gianitsis, emphasized the disastrous policies of the previous government vis-à-vis the industrial sector, its prioritization and hyper-protection of light industry and the turn towards the expansion of the service sector. As representatives of the 'modernizing' faction of PASOK, Simitis and his associates insisted, instead, on a set of policies that would strengthen specific sectors, primarily those of high-intensity and cutting-edge technology, which would be complementary to the development of the secondary sector. Contrary to the policies that favoured the tertiary sector, Simitis sought a different model of accumulation whose fundamental focus was on nationally independent productive forces, the introduction of new technology and a renewed role for the state.[38]

By the time Simitis became leader of PASOK and prime minister, the positions of the modernizing faction of PASOK had been enriched by the global developments of the capitalist economy. It was the time when social democracy reconfigured itself as a 'third way', appearing as a 'solution' to the gridlock caused by old socialist positions (the so-called 'mixed economy', which favoured a close connection and cooperation between state, labour and capital) and the neoliberal positions of Thatcher.

## Three Ways to Hell

Simitis's own positions and strategy borrowed from the almost simultaneous developments of the UK's Labour Party under Tony Blair and Germany's Social Democratic Party (SPD), initially under Björn Engholm and later under Gerhard Schröder.[39] Taking the free market to be an unavoidable and undeniable reality, the 'third way' sought to take advantage of and consolidate the transformations brought about by monetarist policies and the vast expansion of the market. Against the backdrop of the deconstruction of collective understandings of society and collective struggles, the modernization of capitalist society became its epicentre: establishing and glorifying a framework of institutionalized individualism, each person was now meant to be responsible for his or her actions (regardless of social relations), to take risks (in relation to investments and business plans, of course), to shape their multi-layered personality through lifelong 'improvement'. This was the shore upon which the 'lonely crowds' of the 1960s and '70s were washed up, assisted by narcissistic, 'soul-searching' individualized banalities and the transitional period of the late 1980s and early '90s. Following the battle cry of an arrogant and triumphant modernization, which flourished due to the failures of a series of social movements too focused on redistributive demands, the contemporary vision sought to abandon any residual 'guilt' over wealth creation (and inequality) and ostensibly glorified the commodification of everyday life.

This new face of progress, it was proclaimed, did away with the anachronistic divisions between Left and Right and resolutely focused on a process of restructuring the economy to accommodate the guiltless pursuit of (commodified) happiness. In this vision, the role of the state was to correspond to these new demands, to 'decentralize' itself (a process that fit well with the expansion and new role of international institutions such as the World Bank and the IMF and eventually the European Monetary Union), to ensure 'transparency', to fight corruption and truly to serve its citizens. Part of this process was, naturally, the drastic reduction of the welfare state, which should provide 'opportunities' instead of 'handouts' in order to stop the production of lethargic and irresponsible citizens, rendering them unable to take advantage of the new opportunities opened up by the free market. The period when private initiative was 'penalized' was declared over.[40]

Simitis's language at the time was identical. He chastised the 'immobility and sluggishness of the state mechanism' and called for the abandonment of a type of corporatism that gave far too much importance to the labour side of the equation, all at the expense of imaginative and adventurous entrepreneurs, who were the new representatives of capitalist innovation. In his vision, the role of the state would have to be radically transformed, and 'sovereignty' would have to accept its subordination to the forces of globalization.[41] Having successfully fetishized the 'globalized free market' as a set of inherently positive and inescapable conditions, Simitis's role was to 'neutralize' the state by stopping it from being 'torn apart' by sectorial and particular interests, thus rendering the state an effective mechanism for the facilitation and promotion of 'competitiveness' and 'growth'. The question was no longer whether the state succeeded in advancing anachronistic targets such as full employment or free healthcare, but whether there existed an 'effective or non-effective public sector',[42] its performance measured by the degree of integration in the global capitalist economy. Having properly mediated between civil society and the free market, and in the process of preparation for the upcoming monetary union and the modern world of supranational/international institutions, the state would no longer be responsible for creating policy but for coordinating the networks that the new circumstances produced. With a scornful attitude towards old conservative and Left beliefs, the 'modernizers' declared and established that sharing these visions was, from now on, the definition of being 'progressive'.[43]

For Simitis's 'modernizing' vision to succeed, a radically transformed PASOK was required. Careful not to alienate its followers immediately, but determined enough to break with PASOK's tradition, he retained part of its vocabulary, sprinkled with modernizing catchwords. The socialist transformation of society thus became a 'socialist modernization', one dedicated to growth by placing the Greek economy in a strategic position vis-à-vis the European single market and unleashing its potential to become competitive through modernized enterprises, high technology and high-quality export commodities. With an eye fixed on the history of PASOK and its base of support, Simitis declared that this and only this programme was in the service of the People and the Nation.

This seemingly misplaced reference to national pride and patriotism was not, however, merely a concession to PASOK's historical background. Its existence within the vocabulary of the 'modernizing' faction parallels the global attempts to reconfigure the essence and scope of national identity by recalibrating its gravitational force. Instead of an inward-looking and aggressive type of national pride, Simitis favoured an outward-looking and confident business patriotism. His proclaimed goal of making 'Greece great and powerful' was therefore to be achieved through its strengthened position in the field of international competition and the global division of labour.[44]

The enthusiastic adoption of this outlook from private capital was unmistakable. Once again, after 1985, the Union of Greek Industrialists (SEB) found themselves in complete agreement with the aims and perspectives of, well, the same person: Simitis. Decisively attached to the wagon of European integration, they glorified the new economic policy premised on the 'productivity, competitiveness, growth' mantra. The vehicle through which this was to be achieved would be a radical restructuring and improvement of infrastructure, a drastic diminishing of the bureaucratic leviathan (supposedly to reduce clientelism but, in reality, to facilitate foreign investment), and the 'rational' and efficient use of EU funds for promoting competitive economic sectors. At the same time, of course, there would be a significant reduction of public spending coupled with privatizations (or in the more customer-friendly New Democracy newspeak, 'de-nationalizations'): in short, a strategy perfectly synchronized with (and born out of) the targets of the Maastricht Treaty.

Seen as the practical realization of Greece's rightful place in Europe and popularized as a last chance to enter the glittering world of modernity, Simitis's vision swept through Greek society, even as real wages were reduced. There were immediate results: public spending was significantly reduced as public employees' wages (as a percentage of GDP) were brought down from 12.7 per cent in 1990 to 11.1 per cent in 1998, while work relations, especially in the public sector, were aggressively liberalized through the formal introduction of contract, temporary and part-time work contracts. The ultimate aim was to replace the state as the primary employer in the labour market. Moreover, many companies owned by state banks were privatized, while the biggest enterprises, such as OTE (telecommunications), DEI (electricity) and EYDAP (water), were to be privatized gradually by distributing their shares to private interests.

To counterbalance these recessionary policies, which immediately hit real incomes, important steps were taken towards the deregulation of the banking sector, geared to preparing for the credit expansion that membership of the monetary union promised. At the epicentre of these changes were the Europe-wide interest rate convergence and the consequent massive influx of German and French credit. Again, the results were immediate: the banking sector recorded unprecedented profits, 'free' as it was from the vestiges of the (Keynesian-led) state determination of long- and short-term interest rates, eventually transfusing this power to the independent (as of 1998) Central Bank of Greece. Moreover, banks were no longer obliged to invest part of their portfolios in state assets, while commercial banks were 'liberated' from the requirement to commit part of their reserves to the service of government-selected sectors of the economy. The overwhelming enthusiasm over the forthcoming integration was also expressed in the way investors gradually shifted their focus from short-term treasury bills to long-term (corporate and state) bonds. In terms of its expressed aims, the consequences were clear: inflation fell from 20.4 per cent in 1990 to 2.6 per cent in 1999, while the deficit was dramatically reduced and actually became a surplus for two years.

As was the case in all countries, this restructuring process was not monolithic. The transformations described above took place in conjunction with residual non-monetarist policies (for Greece, perhaps most significantly, the boosting of aggregate demand), signifying that they were, of course, limited by the historical conditions and capitalist development of each country. Thus, despite private capital support, the underlying structure of Greek capital accumulation remained largely unscathed, while state-led investment received a boost. Correspondingly, the transformations did not translate into an aggressive curtailment of the dominance of small and medium enterprises – a form of accumulation that can act as an obstacle to massive investments, large-scale infrastructural works and property acquisitions. This setback was recognized by the government, which sought to overcome it by promoting mergers of smaller enterprises with larger companies better equipped to fulfil this role, but the success of this project remained incomplete.[45] Similarly, the Simitis period saw selective wage increases in specific sectors and the funding of some infrastructural works through a combination of EU, state and private funds.

The combination of bank profitability and low interest rates (which expressed itself through increased money-creation by way of loans), a more 'efficient' use of EU funds and targeted increases in wages generated something similar to the so-called wealth effect. But it is absolutely imperative to add that this generalized feeling of well-being was at the same time heavily dependent on the influx of a mass wave of migration, from the former Eastern bloc (most notably Albania, but also Romania, Bulgaria and others). Channelled primarily towards the agricultural and construction sectors,[46] the exploitation of impoverished foreigners contributed decisively to the 'economic miracle' between 1996 and 2004. But it did more than that: it acted as a further symbolic expression of European integration for Greeks who, unlike most of their European counterparts, had never had the 'opportunity' to define themselves (and their well-being) on the broken backs of migrant labour. This specific development, which coincided with an expansion of the banking and telecommunications sector deep within the Balkan nations, also laid the foundations for a Greek 'catch-up' with modern understandings of racism,[47] involving the reconfiguration of the concept of citizenship as one of excluding foreigners, which, up until that point, Greeks had historically experienced as victims and not perpetrators in their own migration routes.

Translated into numbers, GDP recorded notable growth (3.4 per cent on a yearly basis), while investments also received a boost at an average of 7.3 per cent yearly.[48] The growth rate of the economy was 3.5 per cent on average, while per capita GDP reached 3 per cent. More significantly, productivity, at 2.4 per cent, surpassed the EU average of 1.4 per cent during the same period. However, while wages in a few sectors followed this growth closely, they remained below productivity. Simitis's government became overtly eager to reverse a situation in which the state 'ignores the notions of productivity and effectiveness' and to put a stop to what they called the veritable control of important public companies by trade unions, thereby worsening 'services to the citizen'. In any case, as we have seen in other countries where similar developments occurred, the notion of a 'reduced state sector' was more an ideological veil than anything else. The reconfiguration at hand strictly concerned the functions and scope of the state, not its disappearance. As a result, this period saw the reintroduction of the state within economic policy, called as it was to administer and manage an enlarged GDP and to take an enhanced role as a consumer of private capital's output.[49]

Quite crucially, by constituting themselves as the representatives par excellence of modernization, Simitis and his allies defined not only the present and future, but the past. In this context, anything that was described as belonging to the past was automatically branded 'anachronistic', 'backward' and responsible for all that was essentially wrong with Greece.[50] A new understanding of the economy, the state, civil society or citizenship was in this sense consolidated, gaining a certain hegemony that redefined and reorganized the symbolic representation of reality. Like all ideologies, this one had a material basis: the economic 'growth' (that is, credit expansion) that came as a result of Eurozone membership gave the modernizing approach further legitimacy.

For this precise reason, the idea that the foundations for the eventual outbreak of the 2010 crisis were laid in this period, rather than the preceding one, remains difficult to grasp. Like most ideologues, those who still align themselves with the modernization narrative and Simitis's vision have continually argued that it was the incompleteness of this process and the resistance it faced from vested interests that allowed the Greek economy to sink to such depths.[51] This is, however, not the case.

For this is the period when the liberalization of the banking sector took place, with the subsequent facilitation of credit expansion, cementing the notion that credit is the locomotive of economic growth. In turn, this set the basis for the uncontrolled expansion of the banks' balance sheets, rendering them insolvent (not simply illiquid) when credit ran out and in constant need of 'liquidity injections' that eventually burdened public (*and not private*) debt. The frenzy of speculative finance that led to an incredible rise in the stock market index was projected as an indication of 'modernization' of the Greek economy, but its devastating hangover when the party was over revealed it as little more than a process of capitalist consolidation of wealth in ever fewer hands. Behind the glitter of 'growth' and the 'wealth effect' of the times lay the reality of wage and welfare cuts, increased household (and *reduced* corporate) taxation and the savage exploitation of migrant labour. But the recessionary policies met only sporadic resistance,[52] as they were balanced out by the creation of new money (through credit), which was in turn directed towards specific assets whose price increase, as we have already observed, was not considered inflationary but an aspect of 'growth'. And since price hikes only occurred in those areas where new money was being directed, such as houses, stocks and businesses, and not in other commodities, not only was inflation low but everyone had the impression that they were becoming richer. Lastly, it was the deliberate choice of an overall reduction of the costs of capitalist business ('liberalizing' work relations, drastically reducing capital taxation and turning an indisputable blind eye on employers' systematic non-payment of social insurance, to name but a few) that was fundamental in shrinking state revenue, instead of the – repeated ad nauseam – damnation of higher wages.[53]

Despite the dominant narrative, the Simitis period fully instilled the notion that Greece's future was to be forever entangled with that of the Eurozone (its monetarist vision presupposed), bringing forth the still-held belief that any alternative is synonymous with catastrophic collapse. In a twist of historical irony that is still bitterly resisted, however, the economic collapse that eventually arrived in the late 2000s was not the result of some alternative, but fundamentally premised on the self-proclaimed rationality and modernization that these times promoted and glorified.

*four*

# 'Holy Cow!'

From the early years of the monetary union a peculiar, though predictable, imbalance took shape, one that would eventually explode into the 'sovereign debt' crisis of 2010, bringing Greece (and later Portugal, Ireland and Spain) to its knees.[1] This disequilibrium was the direct result of the fundamental structure and aims of the Eurozone, the convergence of interest rates throughout the euro area and the disappearance of exchange rate uncertainty. It also corresponded to what was considered at the time to be the best (or even the only possible) form for economic growth: the expansion of credit.

Immediately after the introduction of the euro, Greece, Portugal, Spain, Italy and Ireland became huge capital importers,[2] with Spain being the largest importer of all in absolute terms. Large financial institutions and banks took advantage of the common currency in order to 'invade' those countries of the periphery in which, due to lower competitiveness and slower economic development, money was scarcer and interest rates slightly higher. As Yanis Varoufakis describes:

> Now that the Greeks and the Italians earned money that could never again be devalued vis-à-vis German money, lending to them appeared to the German and French banks as advantageous as lending to a Dutch or German entity. Indeed, once the euro was invented, it was more lucrative

to lend to persons, companies and banks of deficit member states than to German or Austrian customers. This was because in places like Greece, Spain and southern Italy private indebtedness was extremely low. The people were of course generally poorer than Northern Europeans, lived in humbler homes, drove older cars and so on, but they owned their homes outright, had no car loan and usually displayed the deep-seated aversion to debt that recent memories of poverty engender. Bankers love customers who have a low level of indebtedness and some collateral in the form of a farmhouse or an apartment in Naples, Athens or Andalusia.[3]

At the same time, the interest-rate convergence meant that the credit-worthiness of, say, Greek bonds was the same as that of German bonds. This was not only an expression of finance capital enjoying a lack of fear related to exchange rate fluctuations and depreciations, or even the absence of strict regulations regarding financial transactions. It was directly beneficial for the export industries of strong Eurozone economies. The case of Germany is indicative: not only could its monetary authorities avoid inflationary pressures by exporting its surplus abroad, but the credit lines offered by its banks contributed to the direct creation of money in the peripheral countries,[4] money that was then used to buy the commodities the stronger economies produced and exported. This predicament augments, of course, both surpluses and deficits, but it also generates 'growth' and gives the impression that the economy is booming. Especially for the peripheral countries, although the increase in deficits should have been a source of alarm (especially considering the Maastricht guide-lines), the consensus at the time was to see this as a normal feature of a monetary union that would eventually balance out due to the furthering of financial integration. More importantly, to the extent that money was flowing around, and interest provided good incomes, no one had any reason to complain. Surplus economies were happy to see their exports increase, their banking/financial sector was happy to cash in on bonuses due to ever increasing amounts of credit loans, consumers were happy to get access to the quality commodities of the Eurozone's strongest and more reliable producers, and demand was booming. And even though debt was increasing, cheap borrowing made everyone think that new debts could be rolled over ad infinitum.

Credit thus became the motor of the peripheral economies and a new model of capital accumulation. Taking advantage of the low borrowing costs of the European interbank market and the effective abolition of risk premium that would have been demanded by investors prior to the euro,[5] private companies indulged in investments funded by local or foreign banks, while the state increased its deficit and debt fearlessly. At the level of demand, consumption was stimulated by lower prices and access to loans. Nonetheless, this credit-fuelled economic 'boom' was not identical in all peripheral states, and in order to get a better idea of the specific forms that the crisis took when the credit party was over, it is helpful to examine the differences.

## Pigs in the Market

Italy's economy is particularly important in the EMU, as it represents the third largest GDP output. And we have seen that its manufacturing capacity was competitive enough to force Germany to 'accept' its inclusion in the Eurozone club, fearing that, should Italy remain outside, its ability to devalue would boost its competitiveness vis-à-vis German output. Indicating once again that the famous obsession about abiding by the rules can be easily ignored when needed, Italy's massive debt and its interest servicing costs, standing at 11.5 per cent of its GDP, were ignored.

In any case, lowering interest rates meant that by 2000 Italy had reduced its interest burden (the debt-servicing cost) by half, while its deficit was also brought down below –2 per cent. However, and despite these impressive Maastricht-abiding monetary figures, Italy followed the example of other peripheral countries and utilized the credit expansion to increase its borrowing. By 2010 its debt/GDP ratio had reached 130 per cent, almost the same as Greece's. The difference, however – which has, until now, kept Italy from going down the same road as Greece – is that Italy's foreign debt remains primarily *private*, while its (long-term) public debt is mostly internal (that is, obligations to Italian investors). This, as we shall see below, played a crucial role during the outbreak of the crisis.

In Spain the expansion promoted by the private banking sector resulted in an incredible real estate boom, similar to that in the United States.[6] Traditionally accustomed to the 'development model' of building massive holiday resorts (with the aim of selling them to English or German consumers), the boom in construction fuelled an impressive 55 per cent GDP growth between 1995 and 2007. In Ireland the real estate boom was even more phenomenal, contributing to a 125 per cent GDP growth in the same period. In both of these cases, in contrast to Greece, the state had no direct participation in the creation of these bubbles.

Greece and Portugal also experienced credit expansion by taking advantage of the recently deregulated banking sector, with the flood of cheap French and German capital prompting them to a manifold increase in their loan-giving business. However, the credit party did not create as large a housing market bubble as with Spain or Ireland.[7] Most of the capital that came from the central and northern euro-area countries was pumped primarily into construction (which accelerated during the Athens Olympic Games of 2004, only to come crashing down soon after), telecommunications, private consumption (such as cars or holidays) and business loans, much of which went towards the mass media, urging existing companies to expand while also contributing to the sudden mushrooming of free press outlets.[8] Crucially,

Greece's government debt in the 'golden era' of the euro (2002–8) increased by an almost negligible 4.5 per cent of GDP.[9]

On the other side of the 'economic boom and growth' of the peripheral countries, some core countries were not doing that well in the early years of the euro. Already from 1999, an *Economist* article had characterized Germany as the 'sick man of Europe',[10] criticizing the disappointing performance of the German economy as a result of its inability to reduce labour costs, to make substantial cuts in the welfare system and to further deregulate a labour market that, according to a company manager quoted in the article, 'doesn't really deserve to be called a market'.[11]

France was also experiencing sluggish growth, allowing Germany the opportunity to blame France for its reluctance to restructure (that is, lower) its labour costs and welfare and pension systems. In turn, France blamed the German-influenced policies of the European Central Bank and its strict fiscal discipline, which forbid job creation programmes and state spending. The accusation had an element of truth: the newly created ECB strictly followed Bundesbank orthodoxy, deeming price stability the ultimate and overall goal. In this respect, inflation was kept below 2 per cent throughout the Euro area, while the ECB's low interest rates, which would normally have favoured economic expansion, were, in fact, only 'helping out' the peripheral countries towards which the credit expansion was directed.

In any case, Germany recorded no growth at all between 2002 and 2004. With this poor performance in mind, a discreet proposal was made to 'temporarily suspend' the Stability and Growth Pact and its strict sanctions,[12] something that France was happy to agree to in 2003. In the same year, German Chancellor Schröder responded to the continuing slowdown by introducing the Agenda 2010 reforms, a set of measures aimed at reducing labour and welfare costs, while promoting and formalizing a vast low-wage sector within Germany. In the process of its implementation, Agenda 2010 resulted in the 'rationalization' of the export-oriented sector, involving the loss of many industrial jobs (whose laid-off workers were then absorbed by the low-wage service sector), thereby increasing its competitiveness.

By 2005 growth picked up in the core countries too. Partly as a result of its internal restructuring (Agenda 2010), and partly due to the 'dynamism' of the global market at the time,[13] German foreign trade received a boost. In fact, due to its export competitiveness, Germany's current account balance turned into a surplus: from a €16 billion deficit in 1998, Germany went to a €255 billion current account surplus by 2007. Eager to avoid the inflationary pressures of this surplus, the ever-constant fear of the German monetary authorities, Germany promoted a considerable expansion of the financial and banking system, aimed at exporting inflation and reaping higher returns. By 2007 the biggest non-Spanish bank in Spain and the biggest non-Italian bank in Italy belonged to German interests.

The combination of the credit-fuelled 'boom' in the periphery and the profits of the expanded export industries of the core countries made the atmosphere in the euro area euphoric. Previous critics of the Eurozone publicly apologized for their misguided and hasty opinions, while the common currency proponents gloated. Official statements of the period further pushed the belief that trade imbalances within the monetary union were both a 'normal feature and easy to finance'.[14] Even the usually grumpy German authorities concluded that 'the main problems did not concern the countries with lost competitiveness and growing balance of payments deficits', but those that were not yet 'benefiting from the widening disequilibrium'.[15] These exclamations remained the order of the day for a considerable period. Even as late as May 2008, one year after the credit crunch in the u.s., the ECB's *Monthly Bulletin* nonchalantly mentioned that 'accumulation of internal imbalances and losses in price and cost competitiveness within the euro area [could] also dampen output and employment',[16] but were not particularly worrying.

With the economy booming, the main concern of the monetary authorities (inflation) in check and the competitiveness of the strongest country (Germany) booming, there was a widespread illusion that the party could go on for ever. To the extent that economic growth would accelerate further economic integration of euro-area countries, there would be enough time to catch up to the rules set out by Maastricht or the Stability and Growth Pact. Eventually, the belief went, most countries would restructure their labour markets, would keep their spending and inflation in check and would increase their competitiveness. What could possibly go wrong?

## Across the Atlantic

The euphoria in the euro area was matched by similar wishful thinking in the u.s. Although the 2000s had started off quite problematically with the bursting of the dot.com bubble, the actions of Federal Reserve chairman Alan Greenspan had created a feeling that the economy was not only in good shape but in a position to deal with such turbulence at little cost. His swift decision to lower interest rates from 6.5 per cent to 1 per cent had averted feared bankruptcies, while further tax cuts by the Bush administration gave hope that economic growth would resume quickly. Government spending was also increased and, alongside lower interest rates, demand was boosted. It was obvious that the lower interest rates precipitated increased competition between the financial institutions, which were desperately looking for higher returns, but none of the monetary authorities seemed interested in or focused on where this could lead. For the time being, the expansion of the real estate market and rising housing prices was sign enough that the economy was picking up, following a global trend of 'growth'.[17]

In itself, the housing market boom in the U.S. was the direct result of the long process of deregulation of banking and financial institutions, especially the opening up of the credit market to commercial banks. Prompted by the quest for higher returns, banks and insurance institutions plunged into the mortgage business, accelerating their loan giving. To facilitate this, several 'sophisticated' tools were devised, such as 'debt securitizations' and 'structured investment vehicles' (SIVS), whose aim was to promote the credit business while dressing it in an aura of safety and risk-free expansion. The belief in such instruments was even 'scientifically' approved by leading economists, further creating the illusion that a crash was impossible.

More importantly, the specific nature of the housing market made it ideal ground for expansion. Real estate is quite different from other markets, as its time span is much longer (it can take years from the time land is bought until someone moves in to a new house or apartment) and thus fluctuations in supply and demand are not immediately visible. On top of that, the regulations that existed in the past to safeguard against the creation of bubbles were more or less eradicated.[18]

In the constant search for higher yields, the various banks and investment companies were continually expanding their clientele, to the point of giving out the infamous NINJA (no income, no job and no assets) loans to people with minimal, if any, creditworthiness. But since the debt securitization instruments allowed them to pack these toxic loans together with other obligations and sell them to bigger banks or insurance companies, the bank that made the loan had no reason to fear a potential default. For their part, those who bought these toxic packages relied on their reputation ('verified' by the 'independent' rating agencies) and the diversification of risk that these shiny packages promised. In the end, as Greenspan had already demonstrated when the dot. com bubble burst, if the worst came to happen and the 'irrational exuberance' of the market manifested itself, the central bank could offer its helping hand and bail out any institution in distress. The fragile foundation of all this was weirdly invisible to most involved: in any case, those who had been warning against it had been proven wrong, as the duration of the housing boom exceeded all expectations. On top of that, criticisms were counteracted by claims that previous housing booms and busts were premised on periods of high inflation. To the extent that the modern system of capitalist management had brought inflation under control, the Cassandras of imminent failure were just typical catastrophists who did not understand the mathematical fine-tuning and the algorithms that were the backbone of the expansion. A few years later, the proponents of this 'boom' were proven to be just as unable to understand the maths as their critics.

Those who relished credit expansion and the housing boom responded to critics and sceptics by pointing to the spectacular integration of the global economy and the interconnectedness between financial and monetary institutions. This implied, they claimed, that the widespread allocation of risk eventually minimized it. The irony was, of course, that this was the exact reason why the eventual seizure of the u.s. housing market threatened the global capitalist system with collapse. To add insult to injury, it was, in fact, a very small sector of the housing market, that of sub-prime mortgages,[19] that initiated the panic and brought the global financial system to near-collapse. As soon as the financial institutions responsible for investing in securitized mortgage debt had a sense of what was unfolding, they realized that residential mortgage-backed securities (RMBS),[20] the very same instruments that were sold as the means to secure their investments, were, in fact, threatening their survival. The main reason was that the complexity of the RMBS was such that, in the end, no one really knew what they had invested in. As a result, investors grew increasingly wary of RMBS and then stopped buying them altogether.

In June 2007 the American bank Bear Stearns, the smallest of the five biggest investment banks, was forced to come to the rescue of two of its SIVS. A few weeks later BNP Paribas, France's biggest bank and the second biggest in the EMU, announced that it would stop reselling RMBS, as it was unable to ensure the safety of the investment. Within hours of the announcement, the global financial system froze. Central banks and monetary authorities jumped in and swiftly promised that they would bail out any institutions that found themselves in distress, especially those deemed 'too big to fail'. A similar policy was chosen within the Eurozone,[21] and for a time the markets were 'calmed'.[22] Although the economy slowed down, the sheer thought that absolute disaster had been avoided made everyone quite optimistic. The worst was, nonetheless, still to come. If nothing else, the complexity of the toxic assets that were roaming around the global market meant that no bank or financial institution knew exactly what (and how many) time bombs they had hidden in their balance sheets.

Confidence in the financial system took a final hit a year later, when Lehman Brothers found itself in distress and the Federal Reserve, pressured partly by criticisms about its 'too big to fail' policy and interested, more importantly, in the consolidation of the finance sector in the face of a financial crisis, decided to allow its collapse. Any notion that the central banks and monetary authorities would be always ready to prop up those in trouble received a heavy blow, even if only a temporary one. Only a few days later, the Federal Reserve announced the bail-out of AIG, the largest insurance company in the world, and shortly afterward a massive bail-out system (TARP) was put in place in an effort to reassure markets that last year's panic would not be repeated.

## This Sucker's Going Down

In the U.S., as in the Eurozone, the near-financial-collapse was dealt with by a swift swallowing up of neoliberal dogma and a dive into the world of Keynesian economics. Ignoring the calls of market fundamentalists who proclaimed that intervention by the state or the central banks was hubris, the Federal Reserve proceeded with a massive bail-out and the injection of liquidity into the market. The ECB followed suit by cutting interest rates – for the first time since 2003 – three times in succession (October 2008, November 2008 and May 2009) and agreeing to a €4 billion bank-saving fund. Once again, the targets of the Stability and Growth Pact, as well as the sanctions for not meeting them, were collectively forgotten.[23]

Contrary to the U.S., and following the ever-present inflation-phobia of German financial authorities, the ECB did not follow through with such so-called 'unorthodox policies' and it thus refrained from tools such as quantitative easing (the process of direct purchases of bonds from its various branches, the national central banks),[24] sensing (and hoping) that this would not prove necessary. In any case, by 2009 monetary authorities were proclaiming that the worst was over and the collapse had been avoided. The U.S. authorities went so far as to claim that early signs of recovery were in sight. However, just when this narrative was gaining ground and the 'markets' were expressing optimism, the EMU's worst economic crisis emerged, triggered once again by a very small and largely insignificant member, with an economy that represented less than 2 per cent of Eurozone GDP: Greece.

# five

# The 'Greek' Crisis

The beginning of the Greek saga lies in the small print of various financial papers that started raising issues about the stability of the Greek economy vis-à-vis the recent financial near-collapse. In a sense this was curious: Greek banks were not particularly exposed to the problematic RMBS that shook the financial world. How could such minimal exposure, along with such peripheral economic output and influence, become such a major issue, eventually threatening the survival of the EMU itself?

The answer to this question should be sought in the tectonic changes that took place after the 2007–8 debacle and the form of crisis management that they brought about. To start with, the response of monetary authorities to the crisis was immediate and unconditional support of the banks that had found themselves in serious trouble, due to the previous credit party. The exposure of European banks to the downfall of the U.S. mortgage market forced European governments to increase their deficits (in order to recapitalize their banks), something followed by an initial attempt by the ECB to buy government bonds in order to maintain some stability.[1] But the turbulence did not simply produce panic within that market; it also turned attention to the previously ignored divergence of accumulation models, the structural imbalances of the EMU.

The panic engendered by the financial collapse had put a lid on the credit supply and had forced governments to increase their government debt, something particularly welcomed by banks that were quite eager to invest in government bonds, in search of safe reserve assets,[2] and in order to meet new 'capital requirements' rules. Shifting towards state bonds might have looked reassuring for the time being, but the feeling was that this would soon not be enough. In any case, financial and state authorities across Europe seem to have had a secret belief that the possibility of quantitative easing (an expansion of the ECB's SMP programme) could be generated in case of an emergency.[3] The idea, however, that the problems created by the cutting of credit could be counteracted by the ECB pumping millions into the economy was one that did not please monetarist officials, who continued to treat the euro's fiat status as a gold standard. With Germany leading the chorus, the fear was that expansive policies could generate inflation instead of the deflationary policies that were disciplinary in nature. Moreover, if those countries that had been slack in imposing fiscal discipline were to be bailed out with no questions asked, any pressure on them to enforce the fundamental monetarist values of the Eurozone architecture (fiscal discipline, anti-inflation, minimal deficits) would, it seemed, wither away. If countries in distress could borrow their way out of the recession, they would have even less reason to implement any serious restructuring of their economies.

## Greek Statistics and Other Disasters

What finally accelerated the Greek saga was the announcement by Prime Minister George Papandreou that the financial state of the country was far worse than had been imagined and that the only way for Greece to be able to manage its obligations would be to ask for the financial assistance of European monetary authorities and the IMF.

Prior to Papandreou's official announcement, the financial press had been keeping an eye on the Greek deficit for months, especially after a late and controversial data report from the Greek government to Eurostat in October 2009 had recorded an unexpected increase in the size of the deficit, setting it in contrast to the previous government's report of April 2009.[4] From a modest 5.6 per cent, which was close to the euro area average deficit of the time, the Greek government had suddenly discovered that the deficit was, in fact, at a staggering 12.4 per cent, which placed the debt/GDP ratio at 112.9 per cent.[5] We have already seen how the 3 per cent deficit threshold was devised and how accurate it is for measuring the economic situation at a given moment. Even in those terms, particularly to those for which this number meant either nothing or too much, such an increase was remarkable. Greece found itself facing a vicious circle: to raise money to pay its forthcoming obligations, it would have to issue bonds with higher interest to make them more attractive to investors. Issuing more bonds, however, meant increasing its debt, and the fear was that this process could reach a point where it would be completely unsustainable, forcing Greece to default. That was, at least, the official story. In reality, the fear was that the inability of the Greek state to borrow at prohibitive interest rates meant that it would be forced to default. At the moment, the combined exposure of German and French banks to Greece was at approximately €200 billion. A possible default on these obligations might have triggered further peripheral defaults for a cumulative price of more than €1.3 trillion. It goes without saying that such a possibility would have wiped out the banking system of Europe.

Clearly this was not an option for European officials. But the possibility of increasing deficits even more to deal with the banking sector was already anathema.[6] It was thus imperative that a different path to deal with toxic exposure would have to be devised, and Greece provided the perfect opportunity.

## Useful Idiots

The report of the European Commission on the discrepancies of Greek statistics includes a detailed breakdown of the causes of the increased deficit.[7] Apart from issues related to miscalculated tax revenues, military expenditures, debt assumptions and hospital liabilities, an important upward revision of the deficit concerned the addition (for the first time) of the debt of a number of semi-public companies as a liability of the General Government. But the deficit was not the only trigger for Greece's heroic exit from the market.

Parallel to stories of hidden deficits, the financial press had also detected an incredible rise in the spreads of Greek state bonds.[8] Around the same time that Papandreou made his official announcement about the revised deficit, the authorities that control the Electronic Secondary Bond Market announced that they were closing a 'small window' that had been opened and which had effectively allowed the naked short selling of Greek bonds. The main accusation (formulated as an official question in parliament by a PASOK MP) was that the Central Bank of Greece had extended, in the last four months, the settlement period for bond transactions by seven days, essentially giving speculators the opportunity to push down the prices of Greek bonds before delivering them.[9] In other words, failed transactions (failures to deliver on a promised sale) were not penalized.

Taken together, the speed of delivery of the new official debt/ deficit statistics,[10] the revised methodology with which the new government updated its Excessive Deficit Procedure (EDP) report, and the extraordinary decision of the Central Bank of Greece to allow naked short selling, are hard to fathom. Whether these represent an expression of astonishing irresponsibility or a deliberate intervention is rather hard to determine.[11] In any case, the Greek economy appeared in such a dreadful state that foreign assistance became inevitable.

Deliberate or not, the statistical anomalies led Europeans to accuse Greece of being in breach of EU obligations.[12] With the yields of Greek bonds at 7.25 per cent (3.5 per cent more than Germany's), it was becoming clear that the golden days when Greece could borrow at low Eurozone interest rates were reaching an abrupt end. For this reason, European officials started making statements that a rescue plan was being prepared, specifically mentioning that the IMF would *not* be included. Meanwhile, a very specific chorus began in Europe: statistical problems were the result of massive corruption, while the terrible mess of the economy was the result of Greeks 'living beyond their means'. Around the same time, the *local* chorus joined in, accusing workers of non-competitiveness, laziness, irrational resistance to restructuring and entrenched interests. From without or within, the conclusion was the same: the Greek economy was in trouble and the responsibility belonged to the Greeks themselves.[13]

Here was a golden opportunity to deal with two problems at the same time: initiate a bail-out mechanism that would protect German and French bank exposure, disguised as a solidarity act to help the insubordinate Greeks; and, separately, enforce a massive process of restructuring the economy along the monetarist dreams of fiscal consolidation, tight spending and 'liberalized' labour markets as spelled out by the Maastricht Treaty.

Initially the image of the collapsing Greek economy was presented as something that took European officials by surprise.[14] Only a while ago the world was being told that the worst potentials of the global crisis had been averted, while the financial collapse in the U.S. had been confined, controlled and effectively compartmentalized. How could a country that produced only 2 per cent of euro-area GDP suddenly reverse this narrative and become such a threat? As the story continued to unfold, and as it has continued to unfold, these questions could be more easily answered. At the time, however, there was a concerted attempt to divert attention from the real rationale behind the decisions.

When the details of a potential management of the Greek crisis were being drawn, Germany's new finance minister, Dr Wolfgang Schäuble, suggested that, faced with a possible avalanche of defaults, the Eurozone countries should create a European Monetary Fund, modelled on the IMF, to ensure stability. At the same time, he suggested that those countries that had shown irresponsible fiscal indiscipline should face the consequences of their recklessness, with the possibility of their being kicked out of the Eurozone deserving serious discussion.[15] It seems, however, that apart from Dr Schäuble (and perhaps the Finnish government), no one else in Germany, Europe or even the U.S. sympathized with this position, its usefulness confined to a constant threat related to the possible non-compliance of Greece with austerity. In the end, the ECB also rejected the proposal and eventually Merkel intervened to stop it spreading.

But the situation was deteriorating by the day. Faced with the possibility of a widespread market panic, the ECB started seriously discussing the possibility of following the road taken by the Federal Reserve (and the Bank of England) and implementing a form of quantitative easing (QE),[16] while the head of the Deutsche Bank had a secret meeting in Athens, trying to convince the government to accept a €30 billion loan from the German bank.[17] With violent protests already breaking out in Athens against the announced measures accompanying the 'rescue package', and a level of indecision characterizing the various discussions at a top level, the situation was quickly developing into a veritable gridlock.

The main conflict could be summarized as follows: the sudden blockage of the credit supply mechanism that followed the unravelling of the U.S. financial collapse forced all European governments to increase their deficit/debt, while also trying to put a lid on public expenses, in order to keep their exposed banks afloat. Within just one year (2008–9), the average deficit of euro-area countries climbed from 2.2 per cent to 6.3 per cent, while particular countries had even higher rates.[18] This was not only anathema to those fixated on tight fiscal policies (such as German monetary authorities), but it revealed another structural flaw in EMU architecture: that the monetary union founded on the principles of strict fiscal policies was internally undermined by the possibility that national governments could issue bonds on their separate national bond markets, thus funding their deficit in a manner beyond central/ECB control.[19] The crisis, however, suddenly offered an incredible opportunity: to the extent that Eurozone governments could be forced out of the market and would no longer be able to finance their deficits by taking advantage of low interest rates, the goal of fiscal discipline could finally be imposed on them from the outside.

In this context, and while there was an undeniable necessity to provide economic assistance to Greece (to secure, lest we forget, the massive exposure of European banks against the possibility of Greece defaulting),[20] the form that this assistance would take had to be designed in such a way as to ensure a prolonged fiscal tightening. It was precisely for this reason that monetary authorities, primarily German ones, were particularly eager to avoid a repetition of the U.S./UK mode of crisis management, which they saw as inflationary.

Officially, of course, this reluctance was presented as a matter of strict adherence to the set rules of the Eurozone, but this argument loses any semblance of consistency as soon as these sacred rulebooks are looked at closely: any reference to Article 125, section 1, of the Consolidated Treaty on the Functioning of the European Union, which precludes the provision of financial assistance to Member States, has to simultaneously and blatantly ignore Article 122, section 2, of the same treaty, which clearly states that a Member State that finds itself in difficulties 'caused by natural disasters or *exceptional occurrences beyond its control*' may, in fact, be granted financial assistance. Surely, the effects of a global economic crisis on a small peripheral economy more than qualify as an 'exceptional occurrence beyond its control'. The refusal to admit this obvious fact and instead to cherry-pick the procedural guidelines was therefore pertinent. And it remains the elementary reason why the Greek economic collapse was portrayed, and continues to be portrayed to this day, as the result of *internal* mismanagement and corruption.

The extended invitation to the IMF to join this restructuring party was not merely a result of the consideration that the capital that would eventually be required was beyond EMU capacity. It also represented the need to lend some external (non-EZ) justification to the process and somehow safeguard against the political costs that this austerity odyssey would bring.[21]

In the end, an agreement on how to proceed with the potential collapse of Greece (and eventually other countries) was drawn up. With Greece having no access to the markets, a common fund (a 'Troika', consisting of the European Commission, the ECB and the IMF) would be set up to provide loans that would keep the economy from defaulting,[22] but only in exchange for a drastic restructuring of the economy along monetarist lines: privatizations, cuts in public spending (such as health and education), slashed labour costs, welfare and pensions. The obvious fault in this plan was invisible only to those who were embedded within the confines of market fundamentalism or to those elites who never saw the cracks opening in so-called EU (bourgeois) solidarity. For anyone else, the notion that this restructuring could facilitate economic recovery, paving the way for the incredible joy that re-entering the markets would bring, was simply absurd. Even if one took the official proclamations at face value and accepted that the programme was designed to deal with Greece's chronic mismanagement, bad economic performance and increased debt, the notion that adding more debt while implementing an austerity programme that would predictably devastate economic activity, output and GDP seems to come directly out of some Kafkaesque nightmare.

As the details of a €110 billion rescue package to Greece were being finalized, the general coordinates of Eurozone crisis management were drawn up. For the needs of the bail-out, the ECB and European Commission would provide an amount of €80 billion in bilateral loans,[23] while the IMF would assist with 'technical expertise' and another €30 billion.[24] Exposed banks could rely on ample capital to recapitalize, while their private debts would be magically transformed into public ones, as the 'rescue package' increased public debt. At the same time, using the excuse of a corrupt and inefficient Greek economy, a harsh process of austerity would be imposed that would supposedly allow the economy to bounce back, regenerate growth and repay the loans.[25]

On a parallel level, and at German insistence, another fund was to be set up as a temporary 'special purpose vehicle'. Known as the Emergency Financial Stability Facility (EFSF), this would raise close to €750 billion in a joint effort by the IMF and EMU members to provide liquidity and act as an alternative to any ideas of a QE programme.[26] Regardless of this, and outside the official spotlight, ECB officials started working on the formulation of a potential bond-purchasing programme, ensuring however that such a programme would not be misunderstood as an alternative to restructuring.

The delays caused by this back and forth and the explosion of increasingly militant demonstrations in the streets of Athens, which raised fears about the possible de facto cancellation of austerity in the streets, made the atmosphere extremely tense. In a situation that was 'deteriorating with extreme rapidity and intensity',[27] with U.S. President Barack Obama intervening to warn against a European 'Lehman Brothers' scenario, the eventual formal declarations that spelled out the agreed path of the Eurozone crisis were made. A few days later, the first memorandum of agreement between the Greek government and the Troika was officially signed.[28]

*six*

# Years of Stone

The period between mid-2010 and 2012 was, without doubt, the most crucial in the unfolding of the crisis. During this time, the 'sovereign debt' crisis in Greece exploded as both the implementation of austerity measures and the massive mobilizations against them reached their apogee. It was also the period when the illusion that the crisis was confined to the badly administered and chronically undisciplined Greek circus ought to have been shattered as, one after the other, Eurozone members found themselves facing problems similar to those of the 'lazy Greeks'. But it was also a time when the hope that a social movement could put a halt to the continuing deterioration ran up against a brick wall of police repression and the determination of the governing class to proceed with restructuring at all costs. This failure of the mobilizations against the austerity mechanism not only deepened the crisis and its dramatic consequences, but it negatively set the foundations upon which alternative solutions to crisis were sought – alternatives which, regardless of their political flavour, further consolidated the notion that a happy future could only come from some revival of a glorious past.

For the first few days after Papandreou's televised announcement of the necessity of foreign assistance, most Greeks were in a state of shock. Not only were they unaware of the exact economic predicament – after all, who follows 'excessive deficit notifications'? – but the inclusion of the IMF in the agreement exacerbated an already uneasy feeling. Wasn't the IMF, as far as most were concerned, an institution known for its 'structural adjustment programmes' in the 'Third World'? Had Greeks gone to sleep in a prosperous European country and woken up in a developing nation? Dazed and confused, the first reflexes of a society used to public expressions of discontent did not take long and, even before the exact terms of the memorandum agreement were understood, several demonstrations and strikes were called.

Initially participation in these was relatively small, consisting of the 'usual suspects' who commonly mobilize against government measures.[1] But numbers and militancy swelled very rapidly.[2] By the third general strike, called on 5 May 2010, there were more than 250,000 demonstrators. (To put this in perspective, the biggest demonstration during the December 2008 uprising, whose militancy had prompted some right-wing commentators to call for the need to mobilize the army against the rioters, had approximately 50,000 participants.) While this huge mobilization has stayed in history due to the tragic and unnecessary deaths of three employees of the Marfin Bank when the branch they were forced to work in (and which, in disregard to regulations, had no fire exit) was firebombed, another aspect indicative of things to come has largely escaped attention. At least two hours before the Marfin tragedy, a significant number of demonstrators proceeded to climb the steps leading to the parliament building. The tense stand-off at the top with a small number of riot police was a symbolic representation of the character of the movement that would follow. While it was more than evident that the police forces present were completely outnumbered and plainly in no position to stop the crowd from reaching parliament and, judging by the atmosphere, proceeding to occupy or even burn it, the demonstrators themselves refrained from taking that step into unknown territory, stopping literally inches before the point of no return.

This first public explosion of anger, which included riots in almost all the streets around parliament, was cut short when news of the deaths of the bank employees reached the streets. Not used to such tragic consequences from violent confrontations with the police, people were so shocked that the news effectively put a halt to mass mobilizations for the next seven months. Naturally, the government and all those who believed in the necessity of austerity exploited the event shamelessly, essentially accusing all those fighting against restructuring as somehow co-responsible for these deaths. But these first demonstrations and general strikes had not yet achieved the critical mass they would soon reach. No matter how intense these events had been, they nonetheless involved a minority of the Greek population.

## Perspective Matters

The shocks of the early period receded. The government did its best to demonstrate that the harsh measures would only be temporary and that soon the Greek economy would bounce back, while also secretly hoping that the 'loss of sovereignty' engendered by the Agreement might somehow protect them from suffering a tremendous political cost. These official declarations might not have convinced many, but the production of consensus is never premised on public announcements. With the exception of those who had already accepted that economic restructuring was an inescapable, if unwelcome, reality, the calmness of this period is explained by the fact that most people literally believed that even if it took place, austerity would leave them unscathed. And though everybody knows that 'structural adjustment programmes' always and unevenly target the poor – the Memorandum Agreement itself admitted as much – the period of economic 'growth' of the previous decade had blinded many into thinking that they did not actually belong to this social category. The specific type of wealth creation from the mid-1990s until the end of the 2000s had created a widespread individualist culture, allowing both PASOK and New Democracy to consolidate their rule outside the fear of collective reactions. The unadmitted but widespread belief that these long-standing clientelist connections would come to their rescue, even if the government was forced to 'please the foreigners' and implement austerity, further exacerbated their wishful thinking and complacent attitude. Unfortunately for them, they had neither understood Papandreou's real intentions nor had they paid attention to the details of the Memorandum Agreement itself.

## What do these Troikans Want?

The first Memorandum Agreement between the Greek government and the Troika is a document of significant historical value. It not only marks the starting point of the sad saga of the Greek crisis, but it provides an insight into what were identified as the key structural problems of the Greek economy. At the same time, it spells out quite clearly the scope and aims of the restructuring programme. Reading it again with the benefit of hindsight, we can understand a lot about what has happened since and why it has happened.

An immediate realization is that the Memorandum Agreement was totally unrelated to the causes and background of the crisis and the way it had affected the Greek economy. The striking inability, or indifference, to situate properly the real causes of the economic predicament of Greece is remarkable: the identification of 'growth' as synonymous with credit; the credit bubble created due to EMU interest rate convergence; the insolvent and recently 'liberalized' Greek banks, exposed to over-bloated balance sheets and whose rescue further burdened government debt and spending; and the systematic draining of state revenue due to corporate tax cuts. None of these realities is even mentioned in the official document produced in response to them.[3] Instead, the overwhelming focus was on presenting the economic predicament of Greece as a direct result of its own chronic structural problems, problems only slightly exacerbated by a global crisis, and even then in a reverse way. One can thus read that 'Greek real GDP declined by 2 per cent in 2009 and indicators suggest that activity will weaken further in 2010' (p. 1), further mentioning that the '[global] crisis *exposed* the weak fiscal position' [my emphasis]. Immediately after this comment, and for most of the remaining document, the emphasis is on Greece's severe lack of fiscal discipline.

Yet, even within this context, 'fiscal discipline' is conveniently defined in the narrowest of ways. The only part of fiscal policy that merits any relevance to the situation was the one concerned with increased public expenditure and, as the Greek finance minister of the period informs us in his 2016 book, 'most of public expenditure [is] made up of wages, pensions and other social programmes'.[4] That this purely ideological assertion could not be backed by data from his own ministry was unimportant.[5] This phrase did, after all, express perfectly the official excuse for and the underlying target of the austerity process.

Having set the stage, the document proceeds in a whirlpool of misleading banalities (Greece's weak tax administration is chastised in the abstract[6]) and cherry-picking of data (presenting the inflation rate growth of 2009–10 as indicative of the last decade[7]). Most significantly, however, the Agreement performs an amazingly bold inversion of reality when discussing the reasons behind the recent downgrading of government bonds and the situation in the banking sector.

Here we learn that the collapse in the bond market that sent Greece looking for financial assistance was also the result of a lack of fiscal discipline,[8] while its 'macroeconomic and structural problems (combined with unavoidable strong fiscal adjustment over the medium term) affect negatively the banking sector'.[9] Not only are high wages and annoying pensions magically connected to the government bond market, but, adding insult to injury, the lack of fiscal discipline is responsible for the 'illiquid' state of Greek banks. There is no mention of any credit expansion and bubble, no connection to any exposure to the effects of the global crisis, no reference to Greece's goverment debt increase in order to save collapsing banks. The loss of profitability of the banks was, according to the Agreement, the direct result of the Greek governments' uselessness in keeping wages and inflation low.

One is reminded of the cynical remarks of the former Bundesbank President Karl Otto Pöhl on the purpose of the Memorandum Agreement and its goal of saving exposed foreign banks,[10] an impression that becomes harder to ignore when one moves on to the Technical Appendix of the Agreement.[11] Here the unashamed prioritization of saving insolvent banks while cutting wages and welfare finds its ideological justification: any chance of a return to growth in Greece, which will remain very low due to the fiscal adjustment programme, essentially rests on the 'soundness of the banking sector'.[12] The 'solution' to this problem is also spelled out: the 'soundness of the banking sector' will be restored as banks with liquidity issues will be able to borrow ECB money at a 1 per cent interest rate,[13] in exchange for collateral (toxic loans or Treasury Bills) guaranteed by the state. In other words, the direct transformation of private bankruptcy into public debt.

Having established the guiding principles, the specific form that austerity would take was laid bare: an immediate cut in public sector wages, benefits and pensions; the reduction of the size of the state (to render it more 'agile') and a significant rise in indirect taxes, with an emphasis on increasing and broadening the base of the Value Added Tax (VAT). At the same time, there would be an immediate freeze on public investments and capital transfers to public enterprises and a reduction of the size and spending of local government. In this monetarist nightmare, the Greek economy's long-lost battle with competitiveness could only be fought by enhancing flexibility,[14] lowering wage/price variables and reconfiguring the direction of the economy towards increased investments and export-led growth. In this vision, 'labour market strengthening' would be translated as increased 'flexibility' for the private sector; a reform (beyond recognition) of the legal framework of collective bargaining; a 'recalibration' of collective lay-offs (that is, abolishing pre-existing limitations); the 'facilitation' of part-time work and the establishment of 'minimum entry wage levels' (jargon for lower wages) for the young and chronically unemployed. Lastly, key industries (such as transport and energy) had to be 'liberalized', while closed and protected professions had to be 'opened'. Furthermore, the early stages of privatizations were introduced through the 'improvement of auditing mechanisms' for loss-making industries. Finally, a further spending reduction of €4.2 billion (1.8 per cent of GDP) would come from 'yet to be identified cuts.'

## Nonsense Drives Forward

As the overwhelming focus of the Memorandum Agreement was on cuts for public sector wages, benefits and pensions, the mechanisms designed to sell austerity as god-sent prioritized this sector in its relentless bashing. But this propaganda machine was starting from a vantage point.

We have already seen how PASOK's own Stability Programme of 1985 had banked on the widespread discrediting of public sector employees as a 'labour aristocracy'. But more importantly, they could bank on the real and generalized discontent of Greek people towards their services.[15] The reality of historical developments in Greece had meant that the public employees' sector was, to a large extent, dominated by the armies of PASOK and New Democracy party hacks. Within this context, this sectors' efficiency (from capital's point of view) or its quality of service (from the consumer's point of view) remained largely insignificant. The only thing that determined its running was the subject of its 'negotiations' with its employer, in other words the party that oversaw the state mechanism each time. As a result, a combination of real daily experiences, exaggerated urban myths and the monotonous propaganda made this sector an obvious ideological entry point for neoliberal restructuring. If this restructuring had failed in the past, many would argue, this merely reflected that entrenched interests and clientelist communication between the public employees and the main political parties was too precious to disrupt.[16]

As Papandreou had vowed to proceed with a radical restructuring of the Greek economy, the necessity of reviving the widespread 'hatred' towards the public sector was a crucial step. Presumably feeling that the already bad impression that most Greeks had about the public sector was not enough, he jumped on the opportunity to add fuel to a long-burning fire,[17] with the following statement delivered in a speech on 3 May 2010: 'When the negotiators of the so-called Troika came, they went around all the ministries, asking for the exact number of public sector employees. It was impossible to give them a correct answer. The state did not know how many it employs.'[18] Here was the head of the government of Greece essentially declaring ignorance about a fact that anyone with access to the internet could answer in less than ten minutes.[19] Seeing such a wonderful opportunity, the mainstream media went berserk, indulging in their favourite game of boundless speculation concerning the 'real number' of public employees.[20] Of course, soon after the propaganda machine had fulfilled its role, it was quickly forgotten. And when the results of a census ordered by Papandreou were published, not a single one of those who had been furious about the situation paid any attention to it. The reason was simple: the number of public sector employees that the census found was no different from the number given in the latest report of the Greek Ministry of Interior and, at roughly 700,000, offered no particular outrage.[21]

## The Plot Thickens

The freezing up of strikes and demonstrations after the Marfin Bank tragedy had created the impression that the measures would not generate the generalized social explosion that some had predicted. Combined with the already mentioned impression held by many Greeks that austerity would bypass them, the situation in late 2010 retained some of the calm of the previous months, but a veritable storm was on its way.

The spark came during the parliamentary discussion of the 2011 State Budget, which brought to the fore, among other things, the forthcoming cost of maturing bonds for 2012 and 2015 (a total of €79 billion). This information made it evident that the €110 billion loan of the first Memorandum Agreement was hardly enough to meet Greece's obligations and that, sooner rather than later, a new loan would be necessary, accompanied, of course, by a new set of austerity measures. Meanwhile, the gradual implementation of the restructuring process was bringing home another quite banal reality: cutting public sector wages, benefits and pensions did not merely affect public sector employees. In a consumption-centred and import-based society like Greece, the plugging of the credit hose and the drastic reduction of wages caused a real and significant drop in total consumer spending, which started adversely affecting the whole economy.

Combined with other visible and drastic changes (health expenditures, for example, were reduced by 30 per cent only in the first quarter of 2011, compared to 5 per cent between 2009 and 2010), and the gradual realization that clientelist connections were a pipe dream, the mood started to change radically. By the middle of 2011 the complacency towards austerity was over. From that point onwards, the struggle against restructuring started to be fought at many different levels. In the coming period, a veritable mosaic of resistance emerged, ranging from individual, isolated refusals to collective riots and workers' mobilizations all the way to institutional negotiations, quite often behind closed doors. As such, and although the focus of the remaining chapter will be on the movements that took to the streets and collectivized the anger that the restructuring process produced, it should be kept firmly in mind that this was not the only reaction to restructuring. Greeks were beginning to realize that it would not only be wage labourers and other workers who would suffer from the austerity process. Pre-existing 'social contracts' between specific social groups and the state mechanism had taken a serious hit, and many who had tried their best to avoid being targeted, quite often in exchange for someone else being targeted in their place, had failed. Entrenched trade unionists who were building their careers by keeping those they controlled in check, before moving on to a position in the government, suddenly found themselves outside the game and physically attacked in the street by demonstrators. Privileged professional groups such as lawyers, prosecutors and judges, who had enjoyed years of cosy relations with state/tax officials, saw these privileges threatened. Other professional categories, such as taxi drivers, pharmacy owners or lottery sellers, who had enjoyed (through clientelism) minimal taxation levels, a protected work environment or monopolies, were also put on the spot. The simultaneous realization that nobody was safe from the drastic lowering of living standards made the situation increasingly explosive.

## Searching Underground for a Bit of Sun

In the first months of 2011, and after the uprisings in Tunisia and Egypt, the situation in Spain was also heating up. Eager to avoid the fate of Greece, the government of Spain had begun implementing a set of austerity measures aiming to bring state spending down and reduce the deficit. But social consensus was lacking; as Eurozone's highest number of unemployed gazed at the ghost towns that the credit bubble had created, a social movement started forming that would fill the squares of the biggest towns and start several initiatives, such as the movement against forced evictions, rejecting the consequences of austerity.

Right at the moment when the consensus towards the Greek government was crumbling down at a quicker pace than the various public officials chased by angry crowds in the streets of Athens, people in Greece began to band together, inspired by the images of the defiant *indignados* that flooded their screens: students and pupils who felt the crisis management was destroying any viable future; workers who had seen their wages drastically cut and their working conditions deteriorate through 'restructuring', precarious prospects or unemployment; the sector of the self-employed, particularly targeted as prone to avoiding taxation;[22] small business owners who had to close down their shops and seek waged work to sustain themselves; pensioners who could see their meagre earnings evaporating; all of the above, who were directly experiencing things like the veritable collapse of the health system. This wild mix, united by the desire to resist its further proletarianization, and inspired by the spectacle of rebellious crowds in Spain, Egypt and Tunisia, braced itself and started preparing for a proper fight. And they chose to territorialize it in front of parliament, in Syntagma Square.

## The Beach Beneath

The movement that began in Syntagma Square in late May 2011 and very soon spread out to squares all over Greece (thus gaining the nickname 'squares movement'), represented one of the most condensed moments of the struggle against the crisis, its consequences and management. Many have argued that it did not have a specific aim or demand; according to one's politics, this observation had either a negative or a positive undertone. However, there can be no doubt whatsoever that the masses that took to the streets, occupied public spaces and fought for almost two months to defend them, were directly concerned with putting an end to the austerity policies that were underway. And these policies, as we have seen, were nothing but a systematic attempt to render people's ability to survive in a way that was meaningful to them increasingly difficult.

Despite the fact that the first call to gather at Syntagma Square came from an unknown Facebook account, 30,000 people showed up on the first night. Within one week, the number would exceed 200,000. Contrary to the tense moments of strikes and demonstrations, the crowds at Syntagma spent the first few days starting up conversations, debating burning topics, exchanging life stories. The atmosphere was one of enthusiasm, surprise and hyped expectations. As political organizations and other institutions were busy trying to decode and categorize the meaning of this novelty, people enjoyed the moments away from wannabe leaders and arrogant experts, eager to discover in each other the potential for disrupting a process that had disrupted their lives. Contrary to most descriptions, usually from people who were not there, Syntagma Square had no clear dividing lines (such as the infamous top and bottom square divide): as at any festival or large social gathering, people moved interchangeably from one spot to another, savouring their friends' company, meeting new people, flirting insatiably, taking part in the assembly or having a laugh at parliament and its guards.

Perhaps due to this joyous context, the people in the square had no trouble in identifying their enemies: politicians and political parties that were displaying their commitment to austerity; smaller political parties, groups and organizations that, just like advertising agencies, were, above all, concerned with attracting new customers for their commodity/ideology; the mass media, whose aim was to present (and consolidate) austerity as necessary; the bosses, whose pursuit of profit made them more than willing to celebrate the restructuring process as a means of further reducing labour costs; the trade unions, identified as being the mediation between capital and labour power on the side of capital and its political representatives. On top of that, the Syntagma occupation was, from its inception, a place where racism and the xenophobic sentiments that had forcefully appeared shortly before were *not* tolerated.[23]

What is particularly of interest in relation to the Syntagma movement was that large parts of the established Left, its various groupuscules and even some more radical corners exclaimed an immediate negative reaction to its outbreak that could also be described as Pavlovian. For some, this was somewhat understandable: left-wing groupings that can only sustain any sense of coherence by force-feeding their identity on others (selling papers, collecting signatures, waving their distinguishable flags and memorabilia) were either ignored or forced to leave. In fact, it was mostly those of the established Left who saw in this movement a chance for increasing their voters' clientele and were strategic enough to *hide* their political membership, such as Syriza members, who remained there. As far as the more radical milieu was concerned, their reaction can only be explained as the concentrated result of years of marginalization or isolation and echo-chamber comfort.[24]

In their case, the creation of an identity of radicalism by way of excluding the 'reformist' or 'passive' majority rendered them incapable of understanding that their abstract propagation of social uprisings or even revolution necessitates an interaction and co-existence with this very majority and all its contradictions. This is precisely the difference between a political movement (one that is created and sustained through a network of shared political ideas) and a social movement (one that brings people together on the basis of their social position and not their ideology or morals). To the extent that the austerity measures were directly attacking people's social existence as proletarians or proletarianized, the Syntagma mobilization was a formidable opportunity to engage in and explore the potentials and limitations of class antagonism in Greek society as it is and not as people would like or imagine it to be. However likely it might have been that these struggles would be riddled with contradictions and problems, this is not a matter of choice. A leap into the open air of history is not accompanied by invitations for 'friends/comrades-only'. Rather, it is only through direct engagement that a movement's contradictions and even reactionary tendencies could be identified and fought against; and it was only by trying to be clear and honest about its content and character that its real limitations and potentials could be explored.[25] At the end of the day, presenting the squares movement as something that it was *not* has essentially mystified its eventual failure to prevent austerity and this is, among other things, a heavy burden for future movements.

## Who's Afraid of Anti-politics?

It has been a monotonous battle cry of the established Left of the last decades to proclaim their indignation against what they term the 'disappearance of politics'.[26] Taking a cue from the portrayal of 'neoliberalism' as the process of the domination of technocratic and ruthless market forces against 'democratic procedures', the Left has consistently proclaimed the erosion of democracy as one of the fundamental problems of our times.[27] In this respect, it came as no surprise that many of the Left who participated in the squares movement were shocked (or even disgusted) at the anti-political tendencies present.

One does not need to be a particularly acute observer, however, to draw the obvious conclusion that when the Left speaks of struggles, its primary concern is how to put itself in a position to lead and control them. For such a mediation to

be effective, the necessity of political separation is crucial: in
other words, the necessity of recognizing the importance of
experts, intellectuals, leaders or the fetish of organization.
It is true that, as of late, a certain 'horizontal' structure is
proclaimed by many to be *the* preferable configuration, but
the lack of content of this catchphrase makes it a rather elusive
category. In this context, the Left's attitude towards the squares
movement was not merely the result of their self-important
preoccupations. It was, at the same time, the direct result of
the extensive damage that had been inflicted on politics during
the crisis, the obvious delegitimization of common political
processes. Thus, and while many on the Left applauded the
denunciation of the official political class, the mass media and,
obviously with less vigour, the trade unions, they shivered
when confronted with an understanding that this rejection also
included them. Thus when the popular assembly of Syntagma
included suggestions such as excluding national symbols, flags,
political parties and organizations, many organized political
activists felt – rightly so – that their role was being undermined.[28]

Left-wing parties or organizations have certain advantages
during social explosions. They have better access to infrastructural resources (money for posters, megaphone installations,
computers), as well as a steady supply of members whose
function is to promote a specific party line in a condensed
and calculated manner, hoping to exert enough influence
and direct popular anger towards their own ends, usually
parliamentary. But social uprisings are not merely technical
matters: having control of the megaphones or producing tonnes
of banners and posters does not, in itself, change a given social
dynamic, nor can it easily distract people from the real reasons
that bring them to the streets.[29] In Syntagma's context, the
attempts of the Left (and primarily Syriza) to take control
of the narrative by dominating the assembly, or the smaller
working groups, brought them up against not simply those

who opposed their ideas politically but the fact that their approach and proposals appeared irrelevant to the practical necessities of the square.[30] Thus while there is no doubt that Syriza members tried to control discussions during the assemblies by positioning themselves in key positions of the 'organizing committee', they were hardly as successful as people have claimed in retrospect. It was not only the fact that some of their members were not yet particularly experienced manipulators that proved an obstacle to their goals;[31] more often it was, in fact, the honest portrayal of their vision that alienated people. For example, Syriza members tried to set the tone of the political discussions in the square by organizing one of the most boring events in the square's history: not only was the setting itself in sharp contrast to the usual atmosphere of the square (using a large table for the expert speakers, and chairs for the audience, they reproduced the formal structure of a lecture), but the speakers, apparently convinced they were speaking to idiots, spurted out endless banalities for hours.[32] The official purpose of this grandiose production was to act as the starting point for a campaign that would declare part of the public debt as odious and therefore refrain from paying it,[33] a vision close to Syriza's aspirations but mostly irrelevant to those who participated in the mobilizations. Though the event was tolerated, in the same way that Syriza was tolerated, it hardly influenced any debates.

Nonetheless, while the immediate instincts of participants in Syntagma worked against recuperative attempts, a major limit of the squares mobilization was that its anti-political *form* did not generate a similar *content*. Politics, as a separate and separating sphere of activity, is not only to be found in parliament and/or the official organizations and groupings of the Left. It is, above all, a structurally embedded belief in a certain *process*, historically grounded on existing social relations. Thus, and though the squares movement included the formal rejection of political processes (opting for 'direct democracy', another fashionable phrase empty of real content), it had nothing to say against informal processes. The rejection of traditional political practices was thus replaced by a fetishism of *procedure*, whose aspiration to radicalism was confined to the promise that all voices would be heard. As a result, while rightfully rejecting the lectures of 'experts', the square ended up pointlessly glorifying the monologues of 'non-experts'. The ensuing 'succession of monologues' might have been inspiring in its rejection of the usual,[34] hopelessly gendered, professionalism that one comes across in these cases, but it ended up being a barrier to the practical necessities of the movement, as it became increasingly difficult to reach any decision that could act as a real barrier to the ongoing austerity. What remained was the illusion that words (whether angry, confused or heartfelt) could play a role in halting a process of economic restructuring.

The helplessness felt vis-à-vis the implementation of austerity was eventually compensated by a fetishistic enthusiasm over 'participation'. Claiming its rightful spot in the catalogue of meaningless catchphrases of our times, 'participation' is only capable of describing a 'being-there', while having nothing to say about the content of what one is doing. In the end, as is often the case with fetishism, the term came to mean its opposite: doing nothing while being there. Instead of using this truth (being there) as a starting point for specific actions, a large contingency of the movement felt it was enough to merely declare their presence and moral superiority over those who were deciding their fate in order for economic restructuring to stop. Not surprisingly, it did not.

## I've Changed my Mind about the Mindless Violence

In the end, what played a crucial role in breaking through the comfort and resignation encapsulated in this passive participation was accidental and came from the outside: the police. That was because the cops approached the square in the only way that the police worldwide know how to deal with a crowd: violence. And in that very moment, all those who had invested in the good will and passivity of the crowd (the Left, the media, some hippies) felt terribly betrayed and lonely. For if getting together in a public space and exchanging life stories during a moment of struggle was one link between Syntagma and the other occupied squares around the world, the other was the organized defence against the security forces by all available means.

Regardless of the various attempts to channel the discussions of the square towards the formation of committees and the delegation of experts, the largest part of the Syntagma crowd realized that the only chance to put an end to the restructuring process was to combine the squares' occupations with a general strike that would bring the economy to a stop. The ever-increasing presence of people in Syntagma, alongside the constant calls for general strikes in the assemblies, eventually forced the official trade unions to succumb to the pressure from the streets and call for two separate general strikes, organized to coincide with the specific days when parliament was meant to vote for the austerity measures.

Among other things, what took place during the general strike of 15 June and the 48-hour strike of 28 and 29 June 2011 in effect brought all the monotonous debates around the question of violence and non-violence to a temporary halt. And it did so by blurring the separating lines. On those days, the angry crowd became an interchangeable mix of violent defenders of the square *and* those who ensured their repro- duction: the first aid doctors and volunteers; those who stayed

put in the midst of the riot to provide assistance against
the tear gas; those whose physical presence and loud noises
prevented fear from winning the day. The development of the
confrontations was, in fact, so overwhelming and inspiring
that, at some point, even those who had spent a good part of
the day screaming through megaphones that those who fought
the police were 'provocateurs' eventually abandoned this
pointless expression of respectfulness and began urging
everyone to 'join the barricades to defend the square!'

At the end of the day, the degree of popular participation in
the riots was such that the previously mentioned disappointed
parties (the Left, the media, some hippies) would dedicate an
enormous amount of their energy in the following days to extract
at least some form of verbal condemnation of this beautiful
resistance. But it was becoming clear to many that this verbal
engagement, in favour or against, mattered only to those who still
believed that hearing their own voices in an assembly is somehow
synonymous with social change. Instead, what was becoming clear
was that the continuation of austerity was heavily dependent on
the police, as no 'rescue package' could be voted inside parliament
without tremendous use of state-sanctioned violence.[35] In any
case, reducing the state to a mechanism that imposes austerity
through violence only deepened the process of delegitimization
of political representation and mediations.

It is historically the case that movements cannot be judged
by their formal appearance or even by the image they have of
themselves. This is especially so in a historical period when the
explosion of social media has grossly multiplied and prioritized
an endless stream of *individual* opinions. A more accurate analysis
of a social movement looks directly at what it achieves, despite
what it claims or how it perceives these achievements.

From this perspective, it is important to recognize that
the most antagonistic and substantial results that came out

of Syntagma belonged to a sphere outside the official assembly. It should be clear by now, for example, that a number of practical necessities forced participants to ignore the democratic fever of the political apparatchiks of all flavours and to act in accord with a particular moment of truth experienced by the movement (the attempt to blockade the process of restructuring) and not in terms of an abstract respect for a multiplicity of opinions.[36] Of course, as the Syntagma Square occupation and its corresponding movement was above all a *social* movement, it became the focal point for the expression of contradictory interests and aspirations. But since a struggle is not merely a public display of fixed positions (contrary to what the Left would wish) but a *process*, these aspirations and interests were subjected to many changes while it was unfolding.

Social movements are not only confronted by external enemies. Inside their ranks an unequal dialectic is fought, one in which the past sets its own limits on the future. An attack on existing conditions, such as austerity, brings forth a counterforce that stubbornly rejects this reconfiguration, quite often regardless of whether the defended conditions were in themselves acceptable. This does not stem from some inherent, ahistorical conservatism; it merely reflects the fact that overcoming what is already existing necessarily involves a leap into the unknown. In this sense, it is the ability of a social movement to enforce the permanent domination of the past by the present that remains its most important task. That is because the more its aspirations are shaken by external repression and its own contradictions, the more compelling it becomes to imagine a return to normality as a shield against further defeats. But it is often the case (and it was certainly so in Greece in 2011) that this 'normality' was no longer available. In this landscape, all appeals to a beautiful past become nothing but mythical reflections of the inadequacies of the present.

Understanding restructuring as a process of impoverishment and immiseration, the crowds that took to the streets attempted to use their collective existence as a pressure point against this development. In doing so, they were also forced to realize the limitations of a purely defensive struggle, as those responsible for implementing austerity were gradually making it clear that they would not take a single step back. The decision that austerity would proceed no matter what came as a shock especially to those who were used to a certain theatricality of previous struggles but it also, for the same reason, contributed to the further delegitimization of accepted political processes. Above all, it demonstrated a new paradigm, unprecedented for the heavily polarized political history of Greece: the tremendous flexibility of modern crisis governance, practically translated as the willingness to sacrifice even the most loyal proponents of the austerity machine if that was deemed necessary for the process of restructuring itself to continue.

In between 2010 and 2015, all political parties that were identified as supporting the restructuring process saw their governments eventually crumble and collapse under the weight of the restructuring they helped implement.[37] Nonetheless, and despite this historically unprecedented delegitimization of political representation, the social movement that was responsible (at least in part) for its emergence never produced any tangible option for its overcoming. However interesting the popular assemblies might have been for participants, and especially those who had had no experience of collective struggles, their methods and structure were hardly a sustainable proposal beyond the realm of protest. It was more as if this social experiment was being played out in a parallel world, one that proclaimed its indifference towards existing structures and mediations. And though the rupture with established political traditions was a positive overcoming of a pointless passivity, the movement was unable to recognize that, unless it practically abolishes such structures and mediations, it cannot escape their clutches. Unfortunately for those hopeful demonstrators, turning one's back on existing structures does not make them disappear –

not unless one's subversive activity manages to destroy the material reasons that produce them in the first place. In the end, having failed to undermine the raison d'être of established relations, the movement would eventually force its participants to stop looking at the future and to undertake a virtual U-turn, which created the illusion that the only chance of halting restructuring would come from the past.

The end of the Syntagma occupation came after its violent eviction by hundreds of police on 29 June 2011. To many, this signified that the model of mass, militant mobilizations inevitably ran against the obstacle of a governing class absolutely determined to proceed with austerity at all costs. This realization was the first stepping stone for what would eventually become widespread disappointment, depression and disillusionment. But before this approach became embedded, a rigorous attempt was made to transport and perhaps expand the *spirit* of the squares movement outside the arena of major political events. The result was the mushrooming of neighbourhood assemblies and alternative structures that popped up all around Greece, some smaller and some much larger, which tried to move beyond protest and to focus on some of the most obvious and immediate consequences of austerity.

## Small is Beautiful

A small number of local or neighbourhood assemblies, with a variety of purposes and activities, had already been created during the December 2008 uprising, and a few still existed when the squares movement emerged. As the attempt to deal in a practical way with the deterioration caused by austerity was repeatedly raised during the Syntagma occupation, the neighbour-hood assemblies multiplied and were seen by many as the ground upon which such a practical resistance could be built. Dimitra

Kotouza's analysis provides a glimpse at the content of these assemblies:

> Despite the varied composition and variations in the political discourse of each of the assemblies, it can be said that their activities broadly included: collective non-payment of taxes and fares ('self-reduction': for example, blocking ticket validation machines in Metro stations as a way of demanding free transport, campaigning against the payment of the entry fee for public health centres and hospitals); solidarity actions and demonstrations with organisations of workers and the unemployed; the defence of public urban space from privatisation; occupations of buildings and/or urban space; anti-fascism; participation in demonstrations; a variety of forms of self-organisation and sharing of resources (collective kitchens, clothes exchanges, 'social groceries' giving out donated goods); and alternative economy projects (time banks; alternative money; getting cheaper agricultural produce direct from producers).[38]

An important activity, for example, that many neighbourhood assemblies coordinated was the reconnection of electricity to those houses where it had been cut off because those who lived there were simply unable to pay their bill due to shrinking incomes.[39] This became an issue that could mobilize increased participation, as it could bring together people from entirely different social conditions against the same law.[40] More militant activities, such as the collective looting of supermarkets and the free handing out of the stolen commodities, remained rather small and random as the illegality of the action kept many from being directly involved. On the other side, more localized activities (such as alternative currencies, structures for alternative exchange or time banks) had much smaller numbers. They were quite often more solid and of longer duration, as they provided a legal way of dealing with specific consequences of the crisis and austerity, without, however, challenging fundamental social relations.[41] But perhaps the most important part of the self-organized structures that developed in these troubled years concerns the free healthcare clinics. To properly situate their significance, an explanation of the condition of the health system is pertinent.

## We are all Sick

Free access to health care was formalized in 1983 by PASOK, supported by a mix of insurance funds and state taxes. Although the expressed aim was to extend its provision in a way that would undermine and eventually replace privatized health care, this never materialized. As we have seen, the primary purpose of early PASOK was not to antagonize the private sector but to 'pressure' them to provide the proper 'services' that private capital is meant to provide in a mixed economy. As a result, over the years the combination of prolonged underinvestment and the irrational allocation of personnel (mostly a result of clientelism, as well as the historical prioritization of urban centres) had produced a dysfunctional overconcentration of health provisions in cities. Eventually, what was a very low-cost health system for the public had an extremely high cost in relation to supplies, of which the expanding private sector took full advantage, while maintenance was primarily dealt with through deficit spending and statistical 'tricks'.[42]

Public health was already in a poor state even before the crisis. The combination of regional inequalities and an irrational set-up had created a situation in which 'under the counter' bribes to public doctors was more or less the norm, while the provision of pharmaceuticals, machinery and healthcare supplies to hospitals was premised on a system of overcharging. The result was a free but rather poor service to patients, at a very high cost to the state.[43]

The 'rationalization' of healthcare in Greece by the restructuring process was, despite official proclamations, not concerned with those issues. In typical market fundamentalist ideology, the dominant aim was to 'liberalize' healthcare in order to allow for the 'market' to effect its magic and 'efficiently allocate resources'. No special skills are required to know that a technocratic management whose outlook is determined from the 'market' is only concerned with statistics and costs.

Consequently, the healthcare system of Greece was targeted in a way that can only be described as criminally indifferent to the consequences it produced. Obsessively concerned with spending cuts, especially for sectors historically resistant to privatization pushes, the passage of the Troika through the health system was cataclysmic, producing a 35.4 per cent decrease in health spending within three years (2009–12), which translated as a 40 per cent reduction of the health budget. These cuts immediately led to the closing down of many units, especially in smaller towns, and the drastic reduction of an already badly allocated personnel. The Troika-sanctioned increase of the retirement age and a combination of other factors, most notably deteriorating work conditions, burn-out and fear of the future, eventually led to many early retirements, resulting in the immediate reduction of the total workforce in the health sector by between 10 and 40 per cent (depending on the area). Those who remained faced a 40 per cent decrease in their wages – on top of the extra work burden.[44]

As mentioned, the funding of the public health system was based on insurance contributions and taxes. With both these sources collapsing, due to high unemployment, uninsured work and the inability to pay rising taxes, the health system received a further blow. We also need to take into account that all of these transformations were happening at a time when there was a dramatic shift from the private to the public health sector, as shrinking incomes forced people to seek free and public instead of expensive and private health care.[45] Finally, adding insult to injury, an entrance fee was introduced for all outpatient clinics.

The result has been a veritable health tragedy with women suffering the most,[46] the real consequences of which will only become fully clear in the years to come. But the numbers have made technocrats happy (€80 million recorded savings in medical supplies per year, for example), while abstract notions of improved efficiency, such as merging four of the largest social security institutions into one mega-institution, have made Adonis Georgiadis, minister of health in 2013 and 2014 and an embarrassingly ridiculous fanatic, regrettably popular.

This is the context in which the free clinics began operating, urged by a need to respond to the sudden collapse. Working almost exclusively on a volunteer basis and with medicine, equipment and infrastructure supplied by donations, a considerable number of health workers conducted a remarkably selfless and exhausting struggle to help those in need.

What is particularly interesting about the free health clinics, and what separates them from other self-organized examples, is the unique situation in which the same people who were providing this volunteer service were at the same time participating in struggles at their own workplaces. As a result, they were also the first to recognize, elaborate and try to resolve a very particular contradiction that was ever more striking, the more successful they were.

At the centre of this predicament was a dilemma: the more the free health clinics were effective in treating uninsured patients (Greeks *and* migrants without documents), the less pressure there was for the state to fulfil this role. The assemblies and associations were forced to consider that their work, despite being invaluable and extremely helpful, was essentially relieving the state from the pressure to provide such care itself, thus further accentuating the abandonment of welfare provisions.

Free clinics were never even close to replacing the state health system, but in many cases, and given the ongoing catastrophe, they clearly provided the last possible hope for an increasing number of those who visited them. Furthermore, they were aware that the service they provided transformed the understanding of health services as a fundamental right, which for most had already been paid through their insurance contributions, into a question of charity. When in 2015 a large number of those participating were asked whether they considered the free clinics a form of healthcare that should be made permanent, the majority answered negatively, citing the obvious argument that 'so long as the State exists, it should be forced to provide free health care to all'.[47]

As is always the case with self-organized social structures that appear as a response to a crisis but function alongside institutional structures, the burden on participants was tremendous. The ability to maintain their services, while struggling to resist continued restructuring in their workplaces, was wearing them down. Though some managed to sustain themselves through donations, the lack of funds, energy and time took its toll. Local and neighbourhood assemblies reached similar dead-ends. The importance of continuing the pressure against austerity eventually urged them to attempt to refocus on struggles at a central level, hoping, at the same time, that their experiences could further rejuvenate them.

## Who Dug Out the War Hatchet?

The extent of the grassroots mobilization that the assemblies and self-organized structures tried to facilitate was put to a final test during the next general strike on 19 and 20 October 2011. On the first day of the strike, an impressive strike participation more or less paralysed economic activity in the whole country.[48] In a joyous and rebellious atmosphere reminiscent of the June days, and as the demonstration went around the streets of Athens, it kept coming across office and public building occupations. Nonetheless, the positive atmosphere was shattered by the appearance of a new obstacle that attempted to block the movement from expressing its collective anger: the Communist Party of Greece (KKE). This Stalinist formation, whose only relation to struggles is premised on its ability to control them (and when that fails, shamelessly to slander them), decided for the first time since the beginning of the crisis to abandon its isolationist strategy of demonstrating far away from any other mobilization and instead take a centre stage role.[49]

Though the KKE confined themselves to a mere show of force and an observatory role on the first day of the strike, the arrival of the massive demonstration at Syntagma Square on 20 October was confronted with a curious sight: the KKE had lined up its members, equipped with crash helmets and sticks, with their backs towards parliament and facing the crowd. The uncanny similarity between their battle formation and that of the riot police behind them sent a clear signal: the KKE was there to protect parliament *from* the demonstrators. When a small number of demonstrators verbally confronted them for this repressive role, KKE responded by physically attacking them. The demonstrators fought back, but the fight that broke out was initially confined to radicals/anarchists and the KKE, the latter's behaviour bringing up memories of past street fights. At a certain point, however, the KKE demonstrated quite clearly that its role that day was not confined to its usual anti-radical/anarchist hostility, but was meant to send a signal to *both* parliament and demonstrators that it still possessed the power to act repressively, not only at the level of propaganda, but at street level. In this context, they proceeded to attack the whole demonstration from the side, at a spot occupied by people who were simply observing, without participating in, the ongoing fight between KKE and the radicals/anarchists. This sudden attack from the side, and the beatings that accompanied it, enraged the crowd, which had remained passive until that point. Immediately, most of the demonstrators became involved in the fight.

If the KKE had been successful in defeating the numerically smaller radical/anarchist groups in the past, this time they had no such luck. After several hours of fierce battles, and with the situation getting out of control, the riot police, who had so far observed the fight sitting behind KKE members, decided to intervene and essentially protect the KKE. What had started as a clear KKE provocation ended with equally telling symbolism: KKE members wearing crash helmets and sticks marching away from Syntagma Square, escorted from both sides by riot cops. This formidable anti-demonstration mechanism of KKE members, which appeared to have merged into a single unit with the riot cops, proceeded to sweep the streets of the remaining demonstrators. When it was later revealed that one KKE member had died of a heart attack due to the tear gas thrown by the police, the KKE showed once again how far it would go to protect the established order: in their propaganda, it was not the police who were responsible for the death of their member, but the attacks of the anarchists, who were (by the way) police provocateurs. This circular 'logic' made no sense to anyone but KKE members, who appeared entirely oblivious to the fact that they were being treated with even more contempt than that reserved for those outside the party.

## A Lazy Eurozone

While the concentrated contradictions of the ongoing crisis management were exploding in Greece, forcing the appearance of all possible mechanisms that could retain some control over the chaos, the Eurozone elites were starting to realize that their own propaganda mechanism was receiving substantial blows. The moralistic fairy tale that Greece (and shortly after Portugal and Spain) were the weakest links in an otherwise solvent monetary union started to crumble as soon as Italy, later joined by Belgium and Cyprus,[50] took their place in the club of Eurozone members with a somewhat strenuous relationship to the 'markets'. Shortly after the fierce summer battles that took place in and around Syntagma Square, Italy reached mainstream headlines for facing immediate refinancing needs of €175 billion by the end of 2011 and more than €400 billion by 2013.

It was becoming clear that not only was the dominant narrative of lazy Southerners falling apart, but that the mechanisms put in place to keep Southern bankruptcies in a controlled downfall, such as the EFSF, in exchange for austerity were too small to deal with countries like Italy, the EMU's third largest GDP. A reorientation of the crisis management appeared pertinent, one that was forced to take issue with the lurking possibility that future elected governments with a grudge against the current management might attempt to fall back to 'Keynesian' options and finance their debt through deficit spending.

## You'll Have to Wait 'til Yesterday is Here

Faced with all these issues, and with problems of legitimacy reaching out beyond the borders of Greece, Eurozone officials appeared to take a moment to rethink their 'extend and pretend' policies. Several different proposals came to the surface in the following months: at first, Sarkozy mumbled something about creating a two-tier Eurozone, a strategy somewhat reminiscent of the crumbling fairy tale that the problems of the periphery could be insulated. This idea may have pleased the ears of various fundamentalists, but its relation to reality forced its quiet abandonment.[51] From its own position, Germany began to promote the idea that any further bail-outs, recapitalizations or other fancy moves would eventually have to include losses in the private sector and burden not only the state's pockets. Bond holders would thus have to take a share of the cost of debt restructuring, and any bank that wished to receive money would have to issue vote-carrying shares.

Meanwhile in Greece, Papandreou had already been forced to resign after proposing a referendum that would allow the public to vote on the new mid-term agreement (a further €130 billion bail-out loan) and the continuation of austerity. The Eurozone leadership, clearly more equipped to understand that the social consensus in Greece was collapsing and that a referendum would possibly reverse all the work they had so far achieved, immediately withdrew their support from him, forcing the government to resign. An interim government took charge to establish some sort of stability, ensuring that austerity continued uninterrupted, accompanied even more forcefully by a scaremongering campaign that Grexit was looming dangerously on the horizon.

The person chosen to lead this interim government was a valued member of the Eurozone club, Andreas Papademos, a seasoned banker and deputy chief of the ECB. In his short period of governance, apart from ensuring that luxury cars were exempt from taxation and that a number of criminal charges against serious economic crimes were dropped, Papademos had one essential task: to organize and execute the second memorandum agreement of Greece, one accompanied by a debt restructuring with private sector involvement (PSI).[52]

The new bail-out was calculated at €172.6 billion: apart from the non-disbursed amount from the first programme, at €34.3 billion, the EU would contribute €141.8 billion, through the EFSF, while the IMF would participate with €28 billion.[53] But this time around, apart from continuing austerity, the bail-out was meant to be accompanied by debt restructuring.

The discussion on the PSI restructuring had begun in July 2011, setting an inital target of 21 per cent reduction. That was already an interesting development, since, until then, it was gospel to deny any need for a haircut. Papademos himself had publicly declared such a move as entirely unnecessary, but it is fair to imagine that he changed his mind when more details were made available. For starters, this haircut would exclude any loans from the first memorandum and any debt held by the ECB, only concerning bonds in circulation, which amounted at themtime to €206 billion.[54] The announced target was to cut 53 per cent from that debt, so removing almost €100 billion. The reality was, however, quite different.

Included in the PSI agreement was a provision of €37.3 billion for bank recapitalizations (effectively cancelling out their €32.8 billion haircut), as well as a further €34.6 billion to be used as 'sweeteners' in order to convince private investors to accept the debt swap. Immediately the amount that the PSI was to reduce from the debt fell below €50 billion and, as it turned out, the main losers from this were Greek insurance funds and semi-public institutions, which were forced to participate in any case,[55] as well as small-time Greek private investors who were out of the loop.

As the reduction of the nominal value of the public debt was unmistakably minimal (debt was back at €330 billion within a few months), local representatives of the Troika who claimed to have designed this 'unprecedented' haircut[56] have argued that its greatest victory was the extension of maturity dates and the reduction of interest coupons.[57] In actual fact, the second bail-out and the PSI agreement were crucial for a different reason: first of all, it was the first time that austerity was embedded in the rescue package instead of accompanying it. Second, Greek debt was now governed by English Law, a safety mechanism that would ensure that any potential future default would be dealt through international law (and courts) and not Greek ones.

## Shiny, Happy Fits of Rage

The days surrounding the vote in parliament for the PSI agreement have gained historical significance for a peculiar reason: they marked the last public expression of collective anger, discontent and violence in Greece. At the time, of course, the fact that the strike and demonstration it provoked would be, in effect, the last challenge to the further implementation of austerity was not at all obvious. In fact, nobody was even expecting such an explosion of anger to occur. Having gone through the defeats of the 2010 strikes and demonstrations, the eviction and collapse of the squares movement in the rebellious summer of 2011 and the near-civil war that broke out during the October 2011 strikes, participation in the two-day strike called for 10 and 11 February 2012 was extremely low. The same streets that had seen a minimum of 50,000 people for any excuse over the past two years now held a maximum of 15,000 on Friday and an embarrassing 1,500 people on Saturday.

It seems to be the case, however, that people were enjoying a moment of calm before the storm, as the crowds that took to the streets on Sunday 12 February 2012 were unprecedented. The fact that the demonstration was held on a Sunday naturally made it easier for more to participate – there would be no loss of wages, for example – but even so, the mobilization caught everyone by surprise. Exact numbers will probably never be known, but it was clear that the crowd was at least four times larger than the largest previous participation, putting the actual number close to one million people. The entire city centre of Athens remained entirely blocked for the whole day, not so much due to police measures that cut down circulation, as had been the case previously, but merely because access was literally impossible due to the hundreds of thousands of people. The police were left with only one choice: keep a safe distance from the enraged crowd and gradually push people away from parliament by suffocating central Athens with tear gas. It took them more than fifteen hours to complete this task.

Meanwhile, enraged crowds took their time and engaged in one of the most condensed expressions of collective defiance: high street shops were extensively looted and their commodities shared among demonstrators; banks were smashed and burned; more than eight ATMs were meticulously opened up and their contents given away to whoever was passing by; and, finally, an incredibly coordinated crowd (coordinated out of necessity and mutual interest) resisted attack after attack by the riot police, who were forced by the crowd to stand still (when they were not running away). The use of tear gas, the only remaining weapon of the police, was so extensive that, at some point, they ran out. At the same time, the ugly face of antisocial violence among demonstrators, which had occasionally appeared in the past, more or less disappeared, creating an atmosphere reminiscent of a joyful festival rather than a dangerous riot. Little did participants know at the time that this carnival would effectively be the farewell party of a social movement that tried, but failed, to change the course of history.

## After the End

As the streets of Athens went up in flames, frantic developments were taking place at the Eurozone level. ECB lending towards Eurozone countries had massively accelerated since July 2011 but not, as expected, towards the peripheral countries at the epicentre of 'sovereign debt' crisis; these countries actually saw a reduction in their ECB lending, a result of a shift towards the ELA (Emergency Liquidity Assistance) mechanism. Instead it was directed towards countries like Italy, France and Spain. What this reflected was quite simple: faced with growing fears of economic troubles in the rest of the Eurozone, corporations and depositors were essentially withdrawing their deposits from countries that were considered to be at risk and parking them in countries that were considered safer, notably Germany, which saw a reduction in its ECB lending in the same period. As Italian, French and Spanish banks were drained of deposits, the ECB was forced to jump in and keep them afloat.

In December 2011 the ECB had, in fact, already announced its 'mini version of Quantitative Easing (QE) for the banks' in the form of the LTRO (Long Term Refinancing Operations), essentially agreeing to print money and make it available to banks at below-market interest rates.[58] Banks could then use this money for their overburdened balance sheets and for buying state bonds, allowing governments to refinance their debts by circumventing German refusal to a direct ECB-led QE. As the ECB claimed at the time, the LTRO mechanism passed on responsibility for which bonds to buy to the banks themselves. Although foreign banks would be clearly reluctant to buy, say, Greek state bonds as the fear of default had not disappeared, local Greek banks would be more than tempted to do so in the absence of other options. Thus, the ECB concluded, even the threat of default was being passed on to the specific countries, as any losses would be concentrated on its own banking system and not spread out in the Euro area.

By the middle of 2012, however, the short-lived 'calm' produced by these well-wishing actions was once again under threat. Greece was heading for elections, and Syriza, with its official promise to end austerity, was gaining considerable electoral strength due to the simultaneous collapse of support for PASOK and the anaemic performance of New Democracy. Similarly, France's own election polls indicated that Sarkozy was to be replaced by François Hollande, who had emphasized the need to concentrate on growth instead of austerity. Third, Spanish obligations on foreign debt far surpassed all the other PIG (Portugal, Italy, Greece) countries put together. Especially in relation to Spain, the imposed austerity had destroyed the local elites' hopes that an economic recovery could eventually allow debtors to regain financial viability to repay their loans.[59] Furthermore, as many of the private banks had invested in state bonds as reserves,[60] a collapse of the banking system would have seriously depreciated the government bonds and caused a new round of 'sovereign debt' crisis in the fourth-biggest economy of the EMU.

In this context, the mood appeared to be changing. The reluctance to proceed with at least some form of quantitative easing was becoming a clear obstacle to exerting some control on the continuing crisis and its effects. As such, the ECB (and, even more, the Bundesbank) would soon be forced to swallow their ideological beliefs and fears of inflation and accept the purchase of government bonds. Moreover, the already proposed idea of a permanent mechanism that would provide funds to those in distress, the European Stability Mechanism (ESM), would have to be established to inject some confidence into the markets. And, although it would be necessary to stay close to the rules of the Stability and Growth pact as a means of keeping a tight leash on tax and spending habits, an equal emphasis would have to be put on the 'Growth' side of the pact, with generous investments promoting economic growth instead of merely relying on austerity to regenerate economic activity.[61] These transformations in the outlook of the crisis management were fundamental in bringing about the changes that eventually led to the election of Syriza in 2015. But before we reach the requiem of the Greek saga, we should examine what happened in between.

*seven*

# After the End

A ntonis Samaras came to power after the June 2012 elections and formed a coalition government together with a crumbling PASOK and the help of the Democratic Left (Dimar). If non-compliance with the Memorandum Agreement was, until then, presented by restructuring advocates as a sure path to bankruptcy, 2012 marked the beginning of a period in which, for the first time, a concentrated effort was made to present any deviance from the adjustment programme as leading directly to Grexit (the forced exit of Greece from the Eurozone). With the increased percentage won by Syriza (17 per cent) in the elections and the consequent realization that Syriza might well become the next government, the pro-austerity political parties (New Democracy, PASOK, Dimar), the institutional forces (Bank of Greece) and their allies abroad (European Commission, ECB, IMF) combined their efforts to present the Grexit scenario to people as the worst possible outcome of what was already a disaster. The post-2012 period was also a dramatic reversal of the delegitimization of accepted political processes that the social movements of the previous years had brought about.

Conscious of the fate of PASOK after its full endorsement of austerity, Samaras filled his pre-election campaign with a wide range of anti-austerity *promises*: restoring pensions to their 2009 level; compensating bond-holders and insurance funds that had suffered from the 2012 PSI haircut; increasing unemployment benefits and creating an extra, special 'solidarity' benefit for the self-employed; ensuring that taxation would not exceed 25 per cent of a family's income; stopping wage decreases in the private sector; replacing the property tax with a new fair one and reducing VAT.[1] Nonetheless, loyal to the neoliberal tradition of New Democracy, Samaras also promised to accelerate the privatization process, far beyond what the loan agreement demanded. But perhaps most importantly, Samaras put considerable emphasis on tackling crime and 'uncontrolled' migration.[2] Bearing in mind that this was still 2012, in other words three years before the massive movement of migrants and refugees that occurred in 2015, the political choice of focusing on the 'problem' of migration was clearly a deliberate attempt to reconfigure the existing discourse around the crisis. While 'foreigners' had been blamed for Greece's troubles, this blame was focused on foreign institutions or countries, such as Germany, the EMU or foreign banks, and not on impoverished migrants fleeing extreme poverty or war.

## Nazi Zombies

We have already noted that a particular nationalist rhetoric had always been part and parcel of the tradition of the Right in Greece. But the electoral rise of the neo-Nazi party Golden Dawn played a special role in New Democracy's eagerness to adopt an openly xenophobic and racist language.[3]

This minuscule neo-Nazi organization had existed since the early 1980s, but had remained largely irrelevant to the majority of people in Greece, never numbering more than a couple of hundred supporters. With the exception of the radical or anarchist scene in Greece, which had been fighting Golden Dawn's thugs in the streets for years, hardly anyone had even heard of the group prior to 2010. By 2012, as the unfolding crisis took a heavy toll on traditional political parties, Golden Dawn managed to crawl out of the sewers and claim a spot in the public life of Greece.

For Golden Dawn, small was also beautiful. Exploiting the effects of the crisis on the already impoverished Athenian neighbourhood of Agios Panteleimonas, as well as the strained coexistence of locals and transit-migrants,[4] Golden Dawn appeared as a forceful and no-questions-asked mafia that, in proper fascist fashion, promised to 'clear the streets'. Their well-established connections to both the local (actual) mafia and the police of the area allowed Golden Dawn to spread its poison and inflict its racist violence without any consequences, legal or otherwise. This type of activism, promoted unashamedly by a significant part of the mainstream press, earned for their 'no-compromise' attitude a wider audience and ensured their election in the local municipality in that part of Athens.

Golden Dawn found their long-awaited call to action in early May 2011 when a young father was robbed and murdered while on his way to fetch his car in order to drive his pregnant wife to hospital. Not only did the hideous crime happen very close to the area that the neo-Nazis were trying to claim, but the perpetrators were migrants. Taking full advantage of the event, Golden Dawn orchestrated a series of live-broadcast pogroms against migrants that extended far beyond the specific area. A significant number of other Greeks (and some Albanians[5]) joined them, while the police responded by arresting some migrants! Though this explosion of 'street activism' (a euphemism for racist violence) was halted after the emergence of the Syntagma Square occupation and the new round of anti-austerity mobilizations, Golden Dawn had hit a nerve.

Essentially exploiting, to its logical conclusion, a vision of the restructuring process as a 'national humiliation' – an understanding shared by many on the Left – Golden Dawn offered the extra option of targeting poor immigrants and, in typical fascist tradition, corrupt politicians. Taking many by surprise, a reactionary revolt from below was taking shape that saw an easy target in the impoverished, street-sleeping migrants and an irrational, but sensationalized, explanation of the locals' own worsening conditions. This absurd notion, which so far had been confined to the politically irrelevant neo-Nazis, started to gain national coverage and wider acceptance, leading to a sharp multiplication of racist attacks.

New Democracy understood that the 7 per cent electoral support won by Golden Dawn in the June elections represented a loss from their own ranks. Eager to reclaim its space as the rightful representative of the nationalist narrative, the reappropriation of these crucial voters was imminent.[6] Using a mix of its own traditional right-wing positions and the added fuel of recent anti-immigrant projections, New Democracy went so far in this rhetoric that it became hard to differentiate their positions from those of Golden Dawn: the main difference seemed to be that New Democracy members did not personally engage in pogroms and violent attacks. For them, this was a role best left to the organized state.

For this purpose, New Democracy launched its own institutional pogrom against migrants: adding insult to injury, this took the name 'Xenios Zeus' from the ancient Greek god of hospitality.[7] The crackdown, more often than not in violation of international law, was proclaimed a great success by its creator, Nikos Dendias, for bringing 'safety' back to the streets of Athens, as well as improving Greece's credibility as Europe's eastern border.[8]

## Meanwhile in Europe

In the first months of Samaras's government, the climate in Europe was particularly turbulent. The borrowing costs of both Italy and Spain reached the dangerous levels (between 6 and 7 per cent) that had pushed Greece into the 'bail-out' mechanisms and harsh austerity, leading the government of Spain to ask for a further €100 billion from the Eurozone's rescue funds simply to recapitalize its banks. For Italy, with a public debt at almost €2 trillion euros (190 per cent of GDP), the continued austerity was threatening the social cohesion that was only barely keeping Mario Monti's technocratic government in place. Germany's unvarying position on the absolute necessity of continued restructuring in a form that increased public debt was, increasingly, challenged from different parts of Europe.[9]

At the EU summit in June 2012, Monti insisted on (and achieved) something for which many critics of austerity had been arguing unsuccessfully since 2010: that the rescue of the collapsed banking sector could not continue along the path of transforming private into public debt.[10] He proposed the immediate recapitalization of Italian banks from the EFSF (or, even better, the new ESM mechanism), without the state guaranteeing these loans and thus adding to the public debt. This amounted to a form of financial assistance for troubled economies without conditionalities, that is, without an accompanying austerity programme. Instead of a Memorandum of Agreement that would ensure the repayment of loans through the increase of public debt, access to the rescue funds would be monitored by the ECB, which would perform so-called 'stress tests' of the potential banks. The Italian President of the ECB, Mario Draghi, approved this change of direction, but celebrations over this shift were short-lived. Agreeing in principle, Germany cancelled the proposals in practice by arguing about the impossibility of essential supervision of the majority European banks and insisting on only 'systemic' ones, essentially excluding a great number of German banks.[11]

This last-minute transformation would prove cataclysmic. Only a few weeks later, Mario Monti's government collapsed under the pressure of continued austerity. Faced with the prospect of the collapse of Italy and Spain, Draghi intervened and, in July

2012, made a historic statement that changed the direction of EMU monetary policy: he announced that the ECB was prepared to do 'whatever it takes' to save the Euro currency,[12] directly implying that the European Central Bank was on the brink of commencing a programme of Quantitative Easing (replacing the previous SMP) and purchasing bonds from Eurozone sovereign countries and private companies.[13]

The announcement was met with a mixture of surprise, enthusiasm and disdain. Wasn't this promise, after all, a direct violation of the EMU guidelines and the ECB charter, which forbid the direct financing of troubled Eurozone members? Draghi's response was, as usual, immersed in technocratic jargon that muddled its political background. Given that the mandate of the ECB is to control Eurozone price stability through interest rates, said Draghi, the new mechanism was designed to do precisely that: 'correct' the divergence between official ECB and German interest rates (close to 1 per cent at the time), and Italian or Spanish ones (7–8 per cent at the time). For Germany and its fiscal-discipline allies, the announcement was anathema. Coming at the same time as the creation of a permanent 'rescue' mechanism in the form of the European Stability Mechanism (ESM), which would eventually replace the insufficient EFSF, the fear was that developments at the Eurozone level were facilitating the adoption of measures that would render the restructuring process obsolete. The reasoning was that if the ECB directly bought bonds from countries that were outside the markets, and if the ESM was a mechanism that allowed for billions of euros to be put at the service of those in financial trouble, no country would feel the pressure of the lack of access to the markets to continue with 'necessary' reforms. Such a development would not only facilitate the avoidance of further restructuring, but it would cast a negative light on the harsh fiscal disciplining that had already taken place. With these contradictions in mind, the 'unorthodox' mechanisms of financial assistance were eventually established by making sure that access was beyond the reach of those countries not compliant with monetarist reforms and restructuring.

## Back to Greece

Despite its pre-election promises, Samaras's government indicated quite early that it had no desire to question the demands of Greece's creditors. Thus, apart from continuing the implementation of previously agreed reforms, the Samaras coalition approved the creation of a special bank account into which all repayments for outstanding loans, all budget surpluses and all revenues from privatization would be transferred. Confident in the knowledge that a parliamentary majority safeguarded their wishes, the Troika continued their business-as-usual evaluations: after chastising the delay in the implementation of reforms due to the double electoral cycle (and the poor performance of the previous government), the compliance report expressed an optimistic expectation of 'catch-up'. Further on, the specific report re-emphasized the need for wages to fall below productivity, the urgency to speed up the privatization process (proceeds were still below those expected) and for the tax administration to improve its efficiency. It also recognized that a deeper-than-calculated recession was to be expected, while promising a further €25 billion for the banks.[14]

In the absence of any surprises, new disbursements towards Greece were swiftly approved in December 2012 and early 2013, giving the Eurogroup meeting the opportunity to focus on the new debacle on the horizon: Cyprus. With the dark clouds of financial troubles hovering over the small island, the incredible IMF *mea culpa* contained in a report earlier that year, which admitted to using 'false multipliers' in its (consistently wrong) projections,[15] was more easily ignored by the public discourse.

## Cyprus Hill

The growing belief that the future of the European Monetary Union was hanging once again from one of its smallest economies received another boost in the process of the Cyprus crisis, which unfolded over ten days that shook the Eurozone in March 2013. Among other things, the management of the Cyprus crisis indicated a gradual dismantling of the official principles of the monetary union, though disguised as its salvation.

The sorry saga of Cyprus had begun a few months earlier, when the Cypriot banking sector failed to hide its significant and negative exposure (approximately €17 billion), mostly to Greece, as a result of the PSI debt restructuring of 2012. Given the especially small amount, it was probably thought that a quiet under-the-table deal could settle the matter. The recent introduction of the ESM permanent mechanism, however, and the disputes that it had produced in relation to its promise of the direct capitalization of banks in distress had created opposing factions within the Eurozone, with the IMF observing closely. To the detriment of Cyprus's political and economic ruling class, the conflicts would play out at the expense of Cyprus's finances, adding another nail to the coffin of the monetary union.

Specifically, the otherwise straightforward deal between Cyprus and the Eurozone, which included austerity measures alongside a rescue package, came to a halt when, at the insistence of certain Eurozone members including Germany, a new clause was added: bank bail-ins. In other words, banks would have to complement EU financial help by taking some responsibility and imposing a haircut on big *and* small depositors.[16] This unprecedented demand, in absolute contradiction to EU regulations about the protection of deposits below €100,000, not only defied rational expectations but did an amazingly good job of transmitting the fear that Eurozone officials were willing to destroy all established certainties, such as the sacred cow of insured deposits.

The unfolding drama intensified when the Cypriot parliament refused to approve the deal. The story received mainstream press attention, and the real risk of contagion of uncertainty forced most European officials to duly reject responsibility and authorship of the specific proposal. In the end, the specific clause of the haircut on small depositors was scrapped, but not before the ECB had informed Cyprus that it would not renew its Emergency Liquidity Assistance (ELA) and would proceed to exclude Cyprus from the Target II European inter-banking system. A €10 billion loan was eventually approved, but not without a certain banking consolidation: the Popular Bank of Cyprus (Laiki) would close down, and its small account holders would be transferred to the Bank of Cyprus, whose large depositors and bondholders would also suffer from a 40 per cent haircut. In parallel, an austerity package complete with wage, pension and spending cuts reconfirmed the Troika's Pavlovian response. The fact that the new deal was eventually designed in such a way as to avoid the necessity of its approval by Cyprus's parliament did nothing to silence those who were emphasizing the undemocratic structure of Eurozone decisions.

Perhaps the most important, and almost unnoticed, element in the story of the Cyprus bail-out lay in the measure that would be repeated two years down the line in Greece: the imposition of capital controls. Here, in broad daylight, was a de facto suspension of the common currency among Eurozone members: putting restrictions on capital/money flows brought the unavoidable conclusion that Cypriot (and, later, Greek) euros were simply not worth the same as those of other euro area countries.[17]

## Critique of the Spectacle

As the developments in Cyprus were receding into the background, leaving behind only some headaches to those who felt that the treatment of the Cyprus banking sector would be the new way of dealing with financial distress in the Eurozone, Samaras's coalition government was doing its best to keep up with the requirements of the programme imposed on it. Apart from the continuing downward pressure on wages, pensions and social transfers (such as health), Samaras was also responsible for introducing significant tax changes in the sector of the self-employed, arguing (falsely) that the self-employed had too many 'tax allowances'.[18] The Troika welcomed this initiative in its Second Review, as it had been stressing that the reorganization and efficiency of tax administration was crucial for the continuation of the programme (and for consensus), arguing in the same paragraph that a quick completion of the tax refund scheme would inject 'liquidity to many firms that need to survive'.[19]

But Samaras and his coalition went even further. Up to this point the restructuring process was, as we have seen, primarily concerned with wage and pension cuts, as well as healthcare expenditure reductions. These were the areas on which, despite other complaints, the Troika had consistently congratulated the government in all reviews. At this point, however, following the obsessive assertion that the lack of economic revival and the monotonously 'worse-than-expected' numbers were simply an indication that the programme was not being fully implemented, the Troika demanded a comprehensive plan for lay-offs from the public sector. They thus ordered the government to complete plans for the abolition of certain posts, as well as to establish 'quarterly targets for mandatory exits cumulating to 4,000 by end-2013 and 15,000 by end-2014'.[20] At the same time, the Troika 'suggested' that a 'liberalization' of the retail market would increase competition and work cumulatively in relation to the labour market reform. In simple words, the trading days and hours of shops needed to be 'liberated' from the constraints of the past, a process that would immediately work to the benefit of larger enterprises, which could afford to expand their opening times while paying lower wages, further facilitating the consolidation process and minimizing the 'low concentration of capital' that characterized Greece.[21]

Eager to show their full compliance, and forever bound by their brutish manners, New Democracy and its coalition partners decided on a 'short sharp shock' downsizing of the public sector: they shut down ERT, the Greek National Television and Radio broadcasting system, on a single day, sending its 2,662 employees home.[22] The problem was that ERT had been broadcasting, without interruption, since 1938; not even the imposition of the dictatorship had halted its service. In a show of force that would immediately backfire, Samaras had now decided to disrupt its programmes in the middle of the day without serious warning, leaving viewers all over Greece staring at a black screen. (ERT, in contrast to the private TV channels, was the only broadcaster that could reach the whole territory.)

The reaction to this was massive. Thousands of people left their houses and headed towards ERT's central offices in Athens, where they joined the protesting employees who had occupied the building and taken control of its equipment. The protest lasted several weeks, during which, in a show of solidarity, a general strike called by the main trade unions was redirected outside ERT. Once it became clear to the government that they had opened a gigantic can of worms, they attempted to end the turmoil by offering to 'partially reinstate' the company. The employees flatly rejected the proposal and continued to call on all citizens to join the protest, broadcasting through the internet and through a satellite transmission provided by the European Broadcasting Union. Meanwhile, many of those who had gathered outside the building saw the protest as a good opportunity to revive the defunct movement against austerity.[23] In this context, the president of Syriza, Alexis Tsipras, was invited to speak in the first interview to be broadcast from the occupied station. Tsipras arrived and expressed his solidarity with the movement but, to the surprise of viewers and listeners, refrained from explaining Syriza's programme, as if saying 'this is not the time', and left.

## The Strike that Never Happened

Syriza's curious stance, however, was not that surprising. Only a month earlier the left-wing party, bracing itself to become the next government on an anti-austerity ticket, had already shown how it positioned itself in relation to real social struggles.

In May 2013 the teachers' union, which had traditionally taken a militant left-wing stance, announced its intention to call a strike during the nationwide high-school exam period, in opposition to a new round of cuts. The significance of this strike was considerable, for the high-school exam is not merely a routine yearly examination: it symbolizes the 'democratization' of education, as it is the system by which pupils of all social classes gain access to higher education. Moreover, struggles within the education system have the practical consequence of affecting very large numbers of people, including pupils, teachers and parents. Since the exam is held on the same day all over the country, it is imperative for its legitimacy that the process run smoothly in all exam centres: a cancellation in just one exam centre would be enough to cancel the whole prodedure. This gave tremendous leverage to the teachers. Even if not as many participated in the strike as they hoped, in practical terms it would be enough to mobilize enough people outside one or two exam centres, stop the exam from taking place, and sit back and watch the government struggle to deal with the aftermath.

Samaras's government was also entirely aware of the power in the teachers' hands – so much so, indeed, that they took the unprecedented action of making the strike illegal and promising to lay off any teacher who dared to go on strike. This show of force was not only incredibly blunt, but pre-emptive, as the strike had not yet been voted at the union level. On top of that,

Samaras himself promised that if the strike went ahead during the exam period, the government would resign.

The teachers' local unions, with the direct threat of dismissal hanging over their heads, met all over Greece to decide on the strike, sending delegates with their final decisions to the meeting of the central council of the union in Athens. In the end, with attendance in the local assemblies reaching a historical high, an overwhelming majority of more than 92 per cent across the country, voted to proceed with the strike. It was a clear show of defiance.

When the delegates arrived in Athens to present their members' decision, however, the central council, in which Syriza enjoyed a prominent role, responded in a puzzling manner: while accepting the decision to strike, it claimed that perhaps the conditions for such a strike were not ripe. As the local councils had not voted on whether the 'conditions' were ripe or not, the strike could not proceed. This conclusion must surely win first prize for absurdity in relation to union politics worldwide. The implication was that, although people had consciously voted for a strike that had already been declared illegal by the government, they were not entirely sure whether the conditions were ripe for that same strike. It was obvious that such an attitude was to be expected from union members who belonged to New Democracy, PASOK or KKE, but it was an unpleasant surprise for quite a few to see that Syriza joined in this tango by claiming, once again, that 'this was not the time'.[24]

If anyone spent the next few months waiting for 'the right time' to come, they did so in vain. ERT was irreversibly closed down despite the occupation of the building and continued illegal broadcasting, while the teachers' strike had been called off in an overtly embarrassing and self-defeating way. The two last expressions or possibilities of a mass social struggle, after the disappearance of the generalized movement in mid-2012, had ended in total defeat.[25] Meanwhile, the increasing influence and street presence of the neo-Nazis had forced a large part of the radical and anarchist factions to focus their attention on the necessity of a struggle against the fascists. The accumulated feeling of defeat at a social level eventually led to the transformation of the social struggles of the previous period into separate political campaigns: antifascist for the most radical factions, pro-Syriza for the Left.

## Change of colour

The coalition government was shaken after the ERT flop. The Democratic Left had used the excuse of the shutdown to withdraw its support, and the Troika was growing more and more displeased with New Democracy's inability to break ties with its traditional support base, reflected in an increase in public spending, and the slow progress of the restructuring process.[26] The Troika insisted in its evaluations that fewer than half of the agreed measures had been implemented and kept putting pressure on the weakened New Democracy government to accelerate meeting its obligations. At the same time, changes at a Eurozone level indicated that a relative transformation of the approach towards the crisis was underway.

Germany was once again prominent in this. Fearing the possibility of a withdrawal by the IMF, which had begun (after its *mea culpa*) to circulate the idea that the Greek public debt is unsustainable, and the necessity of legislating a new Agreement in the German parliament which risked further diminishing CDU support, Germany started promoting a plan under which the Greek government would start financing its debt repayment directly through the markets. Should Greece regain access to the markets, it was argued, the OMT mechanism of the ECB would be in place to assist with bond purchases that would keep interest rates at agreed levels.[27]

Of course, given the continuing deterioration of the Greek economy, the notion that the 'markets' could regain their 'confidence' towards Greece was ludicrous. There was no real indication whatsoever that the troubles that had plagued the Greek economy for the past three or four years had been overcome. But perhaps precisely because of this obvious failure, a propaganda mechanism was initiated that sought to promote rigorously the idea that the Greek disaster could be transformed, at least in words, into a Greek success story.

## If This is Success

This success story rested on one idea: the attempt to present the reduction of the current account deficit and the spending cuts as a primary surplus budget. Should the Greek state be in a position to cover its own expenses without any need for further loans (excluding interest payments for previous loans), this surplus could allow Greece to re-enter the markets and finance its needs outside the Troika mechanism.

The reality was very different. To start with, the current account balance did not reflect any so-called 'export dynamism', but instead the collapse of imports due to diminished consumer spending.[28] Moreover, the supposed surplus of the government budget, which could be seen as an indication that the public sector was undermining the private one by reducing spending and investments and increasing taxation, not only accelerated the recession but offered no leverage whatsoever, to the extent that it was not utilized for reducing interest payments. Lastly, an exit to the markets in itself would mean absolutely nothing, so long as the terms of this exit, such as the interest rates of new loans, were detrimental to the economy by further increasing public debt.

Despite such obvious facts, the Greek success story became a self-fulfilling prophecy. Samaras's government issued a five-year bond deal at 4.95 per cent interest, raising €3 billion. The move, celebrated by both European and Greek officials, was heralded, along with the announced surplus, as a clear indication that the

Greek economy was only a few steps from being back on track.[29] The enthusiasm was, in fact, so strong that even Syriza's members fell for it, agreeing that growth was just around the corner but insisting that it should be more equitably distributed.

The fact that this 'success story' was nothing but wishful thinking and the result of a propaganda mechanism that sought to beautify a set of failed policies, soon became quite difficult to hide. The Troika's compliance reports were becoming more damning of what they saw as an increasingly reluctant Greek government, while the economy continued on its downward spiral. The ability of the government to maintain social cohesion in the face of continuing austerity also became questionable: not only did New Democracy have a very slight majority, but its brutish manners – and the revelation that Panagiotis Baltakos, who was Samaras's principal adviser and general secretary of the government, was in an embarrassingly cosy relationship with the Golden Dawn neo-Nazis – were intensifying fears that the government might cause a social explosion, cutting short its term. Losing the European Parliament elections to Syriza in May 2014 did nothing to help.

## Profitably Bankrupt

By October 2014 the signs that European officials were losing faith in the New Democracy government were becoming crystal clear. What most likely lurked behind this realization was the monotonous ideological interpretation of the continuing economic decline, which, as always, was seen as a result not of restructuring but of its inefficient implementation. Despite the government's steadfast capitulation to every Troika demand or measure, the final evaluation that would lead to a payment of €7.2 billion was constantly delayed due to last-minute additions on behalf of the lenders. Communications then broke down, culminating in heated discussions between the government and the lenders about the proposed general government budget. The government's obvious mistake was to take the 'success story' fairy tale for granted and to design a budget on the basis of the optimistic projections of the Troika's evaluations. Thus the newly appointed finance minister, Gikas Chardouvelis, followed the logic of the positive projections and claimed that since Greece was back on the markets, the primary budget was balanced, the recession was almost over, and growth was around the corner, the state could relax its fiscal tightening. The proposed budget was brought to parliament in November 2014. Even though it was based on the Troika's own projections, Greece's lenders were furious.[30] All the wishful talk about Greece's return to stability went up in smoke.

The official excuse for the New Democracy government failing to complete its electoral term was its inability to find a majority to vote in the new president of Greece. The reality, however, was much deeper: the presidency's excuse was only a spectacular political expression of a number of exploding contradictions that were reaching their climax by the end of 2014. Already in July, elections for appointing members of the European parliament had shown that Syriza was the top choice for voters, while the threatening rise of the neo-Nazi Golden Dawn party had indicated signs of extreme polarization on the horizon.

It was clear that both Golden Dawn and Syriza were cashing in on the devastating effects of continuing austerity. Either from a fascist, anti-immigrant position or from one of social-democratic patriotism, the ascent of both parties was based on a common thread: a rejection of the loss of national sovereignty and a promise that, under their rule, the state would regain its position as the central mediation between its citizens and the abstract (and also foreign) forces of the economy. In this sense, both parties were promising a happy future as a return to the past: if Golden Dawn drew its inspiration from the military dictatorship of 1967–74 (with some upgraded Nazi elements), Syriza built its image by embracing the style and promises of the early PASOK of Papandreou (with a touch of Simitis's optimism about foreign investments and growth).

At a practical level, Golden Dawn was never, of course, even close to forming a government except as part of a coalition, something that a small number of New Democracy members and supporters sometimes hinted at. The openly racist and xenophobic mumblings of its thugs spoke to a significant 10 per cent of the population whose political leanings until then were predominantly covered by New Democracy, but its functionality was clearly limited to performing pogroms, stabbings and killings rather than providing the future personnel of a Eurozone government. In the case of Syriza, however, the fact that it would be the next government was quite clear to anyone who was paying attention.

## Close to the surface

There was little precedent for the enthusiasm that surrounded Syriza in the build-up to the general election of January 2015. Not only were various left (and even radical left) groups, parties and organizations around the world salivating over the announced end of austerity, but this illusion gripped the main pro-Memorandum political parties in Greece, the Troika, European officials and everyone in between who also saw Syriza as a direct threat to their policies. The thinking of Greece's pro-Memorandum forces was quite simple: their subservient stance towards restructuring could only be justified so long as it appeared as inescapable. For these ideologues, even a slight alteration of the terms of austerity and its implementation would be disastrous: it would essentially mean that all these years, all these sacrifices, had been made only because the previous governments did not even try to do otherwise. For the Troika and the Eurozone members, the approach was slightly more complicated.

On the one hand, we have already seen the continued use of the argument that *if* the economy was not catching its breath, *if* the promised growth was not yet here, this could *only* be the result of the non-implementation of the reforms. Full stop. The equally repeated critiques of the programmes from within the Troika – the false multipliers of the IMF, the always-worse-than expected recession, the consistent 'over-optimistic' forecasts, the obvious non-sustainability of the debt – played no role in this argument. In fact, it seemed to be the case that the more 'mistakes' and wrong projections there were, the more important it was to reinstate the absolute necessity of the programme. Any suggestion of any possible deviation from the programme's fundamentals, no matter how wrong they were, remained the gravest sin.[31] More importantly, and despite its pretensions, it is extremely likely that European officials were well aware that Syriza could not proceed with any cancellation of austerity as long as it wished to remain within the Eurozone. It was therefore not unlikely that certain European officials could foresee not only that Syriza would take back its anti-austerity rhetoric, but that it might even be in a better position to continue the restructuring process: a left-wing government might have an easier time managing the social explosion than New Democracy. Had the international Left withheld its juvenile enthusiasm and taken a closer look at Syriza's programme, they might have come to a similar conclusion.

## Nothing to Recuperate Here

By the end of 2014 Syriza knew that its election to government was only a matter of time. The anti-austerity rhetoric; the promises to every single social category that justice would be restored; the obvious aesthetic and cultural gap between migrant-friendly Syriza and xenophobic New Democracy; the abstract calls for a Southern European uprising against the powers-that-be –

it all matched the superficial sensitivities of a global Left that, when not engaged in some attempt or other to revive Stalinist/ Maoist nightmares, had been desperately looking for a smooth-around-the-edges democratic symbol to rally around. From the little that satisfied them, to paraphrase Hegel, one could understand the extent of the loss.

Echoing the emptiness of the Syntagma Square enthusiasm, which came from a mere sense of moral superiority, as well as the previous insignificance of Syriza in the Greek political landscape (a fact that was eventually marketed as a sign of minimal exposure to the established, corrupt apparatus), the Left plunged head-first into Syriza's propagated image, verifying once again Ludwig Feuerbach's assertion that 'the present age . . . prefers the sign to the thing signified, the copy to the original, fancy to reality, appearance to essence'.[32] In any case, the majority of the population appeared too content with the array of promises and hopes even to notice Syriza's actual programme. Had they looked at it, many might have seen that, in its most consistent and official presentation during the Thessaloniki Expo in September 2014,[33] Syriza's mediocre programme against austerity was entirely premised on certain key preconditions: debt restructuring, the disentanglement of public spending from the Memorandum directives and the inclusion of Greece in the QE programme of the ECB. Should those 'simple' conditions apply, all of Syriza's other promises could then follow: free healthcare and housing for all; reconnecting electricity to those who had been cut off; abolition of the property tax; the writing-off of non-performing loans; the return of the minimum wage to a monthly €751; the return of collective bargaining; an end to unlimited lay-offs and the creation of 300,000 new jobs. Compared to the harsh restructuring Greece had experienced in the last five years, Syriza was presented (and thought of) as the only way out of austerity.

Close attention, however, would have revealed that Syriza's programme was not *actually* against austerity. The measures

proposed were designed to address the most striking effects
of the restructuring process (in Syriza-speak, the 'humanitarian
disaster', as if some earthquake had occurred), without, however,
confronting the foundation upon which the restructuring had
been based. Thus, for example, Syriza never questioned the need
to boost the Greek economy's competitiveness or to maintain
wages below productivity; nor did they seem to consider the
drastic cuts in public spending as anything but an opportunity
for achieving primary surpluses.[34] They did not even question
the downward spiral of credit/debt economics: their debt
restructuring proposals were, above all, a means of allowing
Greece to re-enter the markets and continue borrowing.[35] But
even without this observation, one look at the preconditions
that were necessary for Syriza to be able to fulfil its promises,
such as debt restructuring, inclusion in QE and a disentanglement
of public spending from the restructuring process, clearly betrayed
that the framework within which the Eurozone 'sovereign debt'
crisis was understood and dealt with was considered a given; what
was at stake was merely Greece's specific (and unfair) treatment
*within* this framework.

None of these issues seemed to matter at the time, and, in
fact, pointing them out was quickly discarded: left-wing enthusiasts
had already found in Syriza a new *deus ex machina* responsible for
reanimating the decimated influence of the global Left. For this
precise reason, anything that contradicted this blissful ignorance
could be ignored: not one of its avowed fans paid attention, for
example, to Syriza's central concern about the threat of losing the
'national character' of the Greek banking sector, a concern that,
clothed in the language of national politics, effectively promised
full protection for the managers and CEOs of the Greek banking
sector.[36] Nor did anyone seem particularly concerned about
Syriza's increasingly embarrassing bridge-building with members
of the elite, some of whom were of dubious reputation.[37] In the
context of the unending decline of the previous five years, these

were unimportant details, overshadowed by grandiose and empty proclamations about social justice, sensitivity towards 'humanitarian disasters' and moral superiority.

For many of those devastated by the management of the crisis, clinging to Syriza's promises was more the seizure of a last opportunity before giving up than a choice. Faced with a barrage of announcements about the end of austerity, and conveniently ignoring all other signs, the most common approach heard during the short pre-election period was that even if Syriza implemented one-tenth of its promises, that would still be a breath of fresh air in the mouldy environment of restructuring. In this free-for-all supermarket of promises, everyone could find something pleasing and relevant to their own social category.

Two worlds collided in the run-up to the elections. One was created by Syriza's promises, its international Left support and the need to believe that an end to austerity was still a possibility. The other was the reality of the situation in the Eurozone, the continuation of the crisis and the true nature of Syriza's economic programme. To bring the imaginary world of promises to life would have meant a direct confrontation with the real world. As the crisis management until that point was not, despite declarations, the result of the depravity of evil Europeans but the putting into practice of a specific ideology of economic management, which was never challenged as such, there were only two options if the Troika were to agree to an easing of the terms of restructuring: either they would wilfully admit to a fundamental mistake in their worldview, or Syriza would force them to do so by exploiting a bargaining position that had been 'ignored' by previous governments.

In this crucial context, Syriza's pre-election promises were ultimately irrelevant. Syriza or no, any Greek government that accepted the framework that set the tone for the restructuring would be forced to function within this exact context, which included the heavy burden of two Memorandum Agreements worth

€240 billion in loans. To the extent that Syriza was promising everything *but* Greece's exit from the Eurozone, and therefore a default on its obligations, hardly any of its promises to the electorate depended directly on the Greek government.[38] Instead of an analysis and understanding of the underlying causes of the crisis, which could shed some light on the possibility of a departure from austerity, Syriza opted for a spectacular show that made use of mythological projections of David versus Goliath, an appeal to the underlying democratic beliefs of a united Europe, an alliance of the 'global South' against the 'neoliberal North', and other such banalities. It utilized every single cliché of the Left, particularly favouring those with least content. In its less demagogic proclamations, Syriza quietly prayed for some European goodwill.[39]

Outside the fantasy world of Syriza's strategists, it was evident that the Troika had absolutely no reason to agree to any fault in the programme. The landscape in the periphery of the Eurozone after the outbreak of the 'sovereign debt' crisis was based on a very specific approach that served its short-term purposes rather well: a lack of access to borrowing markets as a result of non-viable debt, accompanied by massive, state-guaranteed loans to save failing banks in exchange for harsh austerity. If a serious debt restructuring did take place and/or Greece was eventually included in the QE programme of the ECB, why would any Greek government continue with restructuring its economy? European officials had repeatedly and monotonously expressed as much but it is even possible to assume that some of Syriza's own members, knee-deep in their arrogant disregard of reality, seemed to believe that they might even outsmart the lenders. In any case, the elections of 25 January 2015 brought Syriza to power, supported in a coalition by the Independent Greeks (ANEL), an anti-Semitic and populist right-wing party whose only role (beyond ensuring a parliamentary majority) was to provide the government with access to, and support from, the traditionally right-wing and conservative-dominated Orthodox Church and Armed Forces.

## On the Negotiation Table

The announcement after the electoral victory of Syriza of Yanis Varoufakis as finance minister, responsible for negotiating with the Troika, was somewhat surprising. While Varoufakis was committed to keeping Greece in the Eurozone, in line with Syriza's strategy, he had repeatedly written and spoken against the crisis management in a significantly more consistent manner and with a clearer approach than Syriza's own economists. His negotiation strategy was based on a foundation that one would have a hard time finding in any of Syriza's own pronouncements: Greece was already bankrupt in 2010, so any attempt to present it as simply facing liquidity problems was a smokescreen. Because of this reality, the Memorandum Agreements that had dominated economic strategy since that time could only be complete failures, as they added loans to a bankrupt country while at the same time imposing austerity, ensuring that these loans would never be repaid. Therefore this form of financial assistance, which Varoufakis described as 'fiscal waterboarding', had to stop and another path be considered. In Varoufakis's plan, instead of protecting the banking sector and its CEOs and management, who should be treated as responsible for the banks' insolvency, the ECB should assume control, clear the insolvent banks' balance sheets, appoint new management and sell the banks to new investors. More crucially, Varoufakis insisted that bank rescue funds ought to be disentangled from public debt, meaning state guarantees for ECB and EFSF financial assistance. A specific proposal for a form of debt restructuring was also offered, focused on a bond swap with the ECB, while the devastating effects of austerity (the so-called humanitarian crisis) would have to be dealt with swiftly through a new Europe-wide New Deal that would put growth above all other considerations.[40]

The relative surprise that Varoufakis was now in charge of the negotiations also derived from the fact that his proposals, however specific and straightforward, had no discernible connection to Syriza's pre-election Thessaloniki programme or the snowstorm of promises the party had made. At the time, these differences were swept under the carpet of enthusiasm. But while Syriza was busy creating an internal discourse, according to which the stage was set for an uncompromising 'fight' with the 'forces of austerity', Varoufakis was busy constructing the external agenda, somewhat far from the battle cries echoing in Athens. For him, it appeared as though the only thing that was needed was to inject some 'common sense' into the authors of the austerity mechanism, make them realize their mathematical mistakes and, finally, sit down together and devise a new path that would put 'growth' above harsh austerity in a way that would be beneficial not merely to Greeks but to the whole of Europe. Uncertain as to whether he was still a professor of economics or the finance minister of Greece, Varoufakis seemed convinced that a 'lecture tour' on the basics of 'crisis management 101' would suffice to end the madness, thereby clearly indicating that, despite many undeniably correct observations, he misunderstood the *overall* picture: the real reasons behind the existing crisis management.[41]

In any case, the discrepancy between what Varoufakis tried to do in Europe and what Syriza claimed to do in Greece characterized the 'negotiations' between the Troika and the Greek government. Varoufakis travelled around Europe and the u.s. offering assurances that Syriza had no intention of leaving the Eurozone; that no unilateral action would be taken before an agreement had been reached; that Syriza was as committed as everyone to proceeding with a sharp restructuring of the tax administration service, to defeat corruption and nepotism; that a certain amount of austerity, translated into the acceptance of primary surpluses as key monetary targets, was entirely within Syriza's programme; that privatizations were welcome, to the extent that they were effective; and, lastly, that no real animosity existed between the Greek government and the Troika: the goals of increased competitiveness and growth were cornerstones of everyone's programme, after all.

At the same time, the Greek public was constantly assured that the government had drawn its 'red lines'; that no old or new Memorandum Agreement would be accepted or signed and that the end of austerity was just around the corner, so long as the public maintained its support for the government.

Leaving aside the propaganda that massaged the Greek public with a promise that Syriza and ANEL would remain firm behind their 'red lines', which were continually moving further and further away from their original positions, Varoufakis embarked on a series of meetings with French, Italian, British and IMF officials, attempting to test the chances of support for a reversal of German-led austerity. At first it appeared that the strategy was bearing fruit: the European Commissioner for Economic and Financial Affairs Pierre Moscovici declared that the Troika was an undemocratic and obscure mechanism that should be replaced, while French Finance Minister Michel Sapin confirmed that growth should be the primary focus of any new agreement with Greece. Italy's Matteo Renzi also made similar positive comments, promising 'bilateral cooperation in all international contexts'. Naturally, though Varoufakis seems to have missed the memo, none of these statements reflected anything concrete, as Syriza claimed, nor did their 'support' in any way preclude the continuation of structural reforms. In reality, the attitude of the 'supportive' governments derived from their own political and economic agendas. At the time, however, the only thing that seemed to be important was beyond those details. What was crucial in these introductory talks was some minimal assurance that Greece would not appear isolated when the time came for Varoufakis to meet with Germany's finance minister, Wolfgang Schäuble, and Mario Draghi, head of the ECB.

The fact that these 'assurances' and positive comments were a pointless and empty gesture became clear as soon as Varoufakis did, in fact, go to Berlin and Frankfurt. Wasting no time in pleasant exchanges, the German government monotonously repeated its position: there would be no discussion whatsoever about debt restructuring, about discontinuing the existing programme or changing anything in the fundamental framework of the agreements with Greece. Draghi was no less explicit: Varoufakis's plan for increasing the amount of Treasury bills accepted by the ECB, as a form of giving the Greek government some breathing space, was out of the question, and any 'negotiation' would be premised on the completion of the final review of the existing programme.[42]

One can say, with added retrospective certainty, that Syriza's final capitulation in the summer of 2015 was entirely foreseeable from the very first days of its ascension to power, when the Troika reaffirmed its clear, invariant positions. What followed after these early February days can only be accurately described as a consistent step-by-step retreat on every single issue, up until the onslaught of the third Memorandum Agreement that Syriza ended up signing. At first it was the demand for some form of debt restructuring that got the axe; soon after, Varoufakis's proclamations that the Memorandum Agreements were entirely faulty and destructive was replaced by an admission that 70 per cent of the reforms advocated by the Troika were correct. A while later, even the despised notion of an extension of the existing programme was happily swallowed, while the sustainability of the public debt and the commitment for a full repayment of Greece's financial obligations were also officially confirmed by the Greek government.

Eventually, when 'negotiations' with the Eurogroup concluded in late February 2015, the only thing that Varoufakis and Syriza had achieved was a four-month extension of the existing programme, during which Syriza was supposed to present an alternative austerity programme. Crucially, no disbursements accompanied this extension, ensuring that any new proposals would be devised in an environment of fiscal asphyxiation and the gradual emptying of both the state's coffers and bank reserves.[43]

## Referendum and Capitulation

The contradictions that resulted from this early capitulation were played out in full during the four-month temporary extension of the programme. Inside Greece the government continued to claim that it was preparing an alternative set of policies based on their 'red lines'. But all the meetings with Eurozone officials and other financial authorities outside Greece produced nothing but rejections. Varoufakis's barrage of inconsistencies and a concerted deconstruction of his reliability eventually became too much for the government to bear:[44] citing the growing dissatisfaction with him, Syriza essentially sidelined him, though it used the image of official European contempt towards him as a means to keep alive the illusion that 'harsh negotiations' were taking place.

From that point on the government's sole purpose was to present the result of the 'negotiations' with the Troika – in effect, Syriza's capitulation – as some form of 'victory'. Making use of an array of 'leaked' documents that supposedly represented the harsh positions of the Troika, Syriza countered with its own 'milder' proposals. In the confusion of the ensuing back and forth, Syriza attempted to mask the fact that its proposals were identical with, if not worse than, the Memorandum Agreements of the past, randomly sprinkled with some excruciatingly vague promises related to growth and the public debt. Having painfully realized that all the preconditions upon which Syriza had based its hopes of a slight change of course (such as a favourable treatment by the ECB, an alliance with Italy and France, and the isolation of Germany), were entirely absent, the remaining task of the government was the presentation of any eventual deal as an 'honourable compromise', a task facilitated by an orchestrated escalation.

This is the only context within which Alexis Tsipras's call for a referendum on 27 June 2015 can be understood. Gridlocked by Syriza's narrative of seeking an alternative to austerity, the appeal to a public referendum was meant to validate the government's democratic credentials and reinforce the illusion that harsh negotiations were taking place. At the same time, the government made sure that the preposterous vagueness of the referendum would force an interpretation as one for or against continued membership in the Eurozone.[45] Convinced that, faced with this catastrophic option, Greeks would choose the safe option, Syriza was betting on an outcome that would democratically and unambiguously justify their own capitulation.[46] This conviction about the outcome was so obvious that the government's official advocacy of the 'No' vote was never accompanied by any preparation whatsoever for the consequences of such a result. When the ECB proceeded with a repeat of the lesson learned in Cyprus and restricted access of the Greek banking sector to the Emergency Liquidity Assistance (ELA) mechanism, forcing the imposition of capital controls to avoid massive deposit outflows, Syriza must have felt even more reassured.

Accepting the inevitability of the monetary Alcatraz of the Eurozone did not, however, mean that Greeks, when asked for their opinion, would publicly celebrate the terms of their imprisonment. The hysterical propaganda machine that was put in place by every Eurozone, IMF and Greek supporter of the restructuring process, presenting a 'No' vote as voluntary participation in a Satanic ritual meant to establish hell on earth, generated such an extreme polarization that it eventually backfired: instead of producing fear and compromise, it provoked defiance.[47] To the absolute surprise of everyone involved, and the obvious disappointment of the government, the vote count showed an outstanding 'No' victory at more than 61 per cent.

As soon as the initial shock receded, government-sanctioned surrealism reigned. While officially and grudgingly accepting the result, the government followed up as if 'Yes' had won. Practically ignoring any possible interpretation of the rediscovered obscurity of the referendum question, the government reached an agreement with the Troika, the coordinates of which were, by all possible interpretations, even worse than the original ones.[48] Not only did Syriza agree to the uninterrupted continuation of the restructuring process and its latest set of measures, with further pensions cuts and a VAT increase, it also accepted their acceleration. As part of a long list of new measures, house appropriations were added to the agenda for the first time. From now on, the privatization process would be based on the German unification *Treuhand* model, setting up a special agency responsible for the privatization of fixed capital and state property.[49] Above all, a mechanism of 'automatic cuts' would be installed, to be activated in the case of failed fiscal goals, such as a 3.5 per cent primary surplus per year. In a desperately embarrassing attempt to pretend that some residue of its previous anti-austerity position was still alive, Syriza called for the mobilization of people against the measures on which they were voting in parliament. Trying to promote the new agreement as an 'honourable compromise', they informed the stunned public that 'negotiations would continue indefinitely' (obviously modelled on the non-negotiations in which they had been involved until that point), while at the same time assuring them that discussions on debt restructuring had not been abandoned but simply postponed.[50] Parallel to these absurdities, they condemned their own pre-election Thessaloniki Programme as 'unrealistic' and 'arrogant' and proceeded to make Varoufakis, who had resigned a day after the referendum result, a scapegoat for everything that had gone wrong.[51] Above all else, Syriza joined the long list of Greek political parties that condoned, pursued and implemented austerity. In doing so, it unashamedly copied the official language that accompanied austerity until then: capitulation to the Troika's demands was, for Syriza as well, a one-way street if one wished to avoid a disorderly bankruptcy.

The option of an orderly one, however, regarded by some as the only real leverage and negotiating weapon that Greece had in its possession, was never discussed.

## Who wants Grexit?

After explaining that internal depreciation is a very painful process, the IMF argued in a supplement to its Country Report for Greece in March 2012 that, even if all variables are in the right place, 'restoring competitiveness by way of internal devaluation has proved to be a difficult undertaking with very few successes'. In any case, adjustment 'works predominantly through import compression rather than an expansion of exports'. To conclude, referring to the experience of Argentina in 1998–2002, the IMF noted that 'an economy can be trapped in a downward spiral in which adjustment through internal devaluation eventually proves impossible, and the only way to an eventual recovery remains default and the abandoning of the exchange rate peg'.[52]

This conclusion was strikingly similar to the position held by Hans Werner Sinn, a renowned economist, president of the Ifo Institute for Economic Research and adviser to the German finance ministry of Wolfgang Schäuble. After several articles, Sinn elaborated his position on the Eurocrisis in his book *The Euro Trap* (2014), explaining, among other things, that the only way for the Greek economy to resume growth was to re-appropriate the most crucial monetary tool that membership of the Eurozone had deprived them of: currency devaluation. This re-appropriation would only be feasible, of course, if Greece exited the Eurozone. Greece could then devalue its own currency, make exports competitive and reduce imports (as they would become more expensive), thus rebalancing the trade current account. In the absence of this, internal devaluation would simply spiral the Greek economy deeper and deeper into recession, forcing, in Sinn's view, well-performing economies such as Germany to provide large amounts of money to keep Greece afloat. Sinn does not mention default, which would imply accepting the non-repayment of loans granted by Germany, but since German exposure to Greece's debt had already been seriously reduced by his book's publication, he did argue in favour of some form of debt restructuring.[53]

Interestingly, the ideas proposed by both the IMF and Sinn are almost identical to the positions promoted by some Greek commentators (mostly, but not exclusively, from the Left), who have been arguing that only an exit from the Eurozone could put an end to austerity.

Discussions about the possibility of Greece leaving the European Monetary Union had already been raised in 2010. European officials, aware that the implementation of harsh austerity would face considerable resistance, also considered the Grexit card, but primarily its use as a threat. In any case, either Greece would fail to implement the necessary fiscal consolidation, and could thus potentially be forced to exit the Eurozone, or it would succeed in implementing most of these harsh measures, but the process would be so devastating that Greeks would opt to abandon the monetary union in search of a breath of air.

Around the second half of 2011, when the social movement against austerity was reaching its climax, some economists and political groupings with a particularly patriotic reading of the crisis and its management tried to take advantage of the polarization produced by the restructuring process and lashed out against the EU, calling for Grexit as the best possible way to end mounting misery. Despite their efforts, however, few of those who participated in and supported the struggles were particularly attracted to the idea. Leaving aside the cultural and historical symbolism that most Greeks attached to being part of the process of European unification, the pro-Grexit approach was rendered even more unattractive by the simple fact that it was consistently used as a threat by the Troika and Greek allies. In this context, Grexit was monotonously construed as a veritable doomsday scenario, from which the benevolent Europeans were saving Greece every time a new round of austerity was imposed. At the time, the most common understanding of Grexit was that if it ever occurred, Greece would not have chosen it but been condemned to it.

After the acceptance of the second Memorandum Agreement in 2012, the uninterrupted continuation of austere economic policies had drained some of the power carried by the Grexit threat. Austerity, which was constantly presented as the unavoidable scenario, had already brought a sizeable number of people to their absolute limits: with youth unemployment close to 60 per cent, purchasing power destroyed, a healthcare system in ruins and the promise of a return to economic stability steadily discredited, the voices portraying exit from the Eurozone as more favourable or at least equally restrictive, but with some positive potential, started multiplying.[54] The disassociation experienced between the optimistic projections of the Troika and the Greek government, on the one hand, and the obvious worsening of living conditions, on the other, rightly generated the conviction that more restructuring was a downward spiral from which it was impossible to escape. Even former supporters found the assertion, repeated ad nauseam, that the problem lay with the incomplete or slow implementation of reforms was becoming impossible to maintain in the face of such collapse.

To the frustration of the pro-Grexit voices, however, the option to abandon the Eurozone never reached a critical mass. For many, the explanation for this was the relentless propaganda that instilled fear and confusion. It was, in other words, purely an ideological matter. As soon as pro-Grexiters were given an opportunity to explain their plans, it was argued, the majority would surely come to terms with the necessity of the project and would swiftly abandon both their fears and the Eurozone prison.

The pro-Grexit camp's lack of success, however, cannot be reduced to mere ideological manipulation. Regardless of the undeniable reality that the recent history of Greece, especially during the Simitis period, had formally conjoined within the national narrative the goal of economic growth (real or not) with Eurozone membership, what pro-Grexit supporters failed to realize was a simpler position shared by many: that an exit from the monetary union carried no guarantee whatsoever of a better life. The deep delegitimization of authority that had swept through the consensus-producing web of Greek society had understandably taken its toll on all 'experts'. Economists and other intellectuals might appear to impress people with their 'knowledge', but this rarely translates into trust or blind faith. Beyond the jargon of economic data and the way experts get to 'torture them until they confess', people in Greece possess the practical intelligence to understand that the majority of commodities with which they have identified any notion of well-being are imported and would therefore be out of reach after a currency devaluation. This realization often led to the next step, which recognized that even less fancy commodities would become more scarce after a Grexit, such as petrol, medical machinery, even food: in short, anything that is crucial, without being a luxury, and that is not produced in Greece.

Without a doubt, the explosion of social antagonisms and open conflict with capital's interests brings forward, or *should* bring forward, an overall reconsideration of what type of life people want to live; even further, it demands an understanding of which structures of a system in crisis need to be abolished in order for a new form of social relations to flourish. But the most vocal advocates of Grexit never engaged in such considerations. Instead, politicians that they were, they joined the long queue of those who premised a happy future in some version of the past: whether this was found in Andreas Papandreou's 1980s PASOK or some beautified version of the Eastern bloc, the pro-Grexit exponents never understood that what they presented as new and innovative was nothing more than an old recipe that historical and material developments have rendered obsolete.

## Groundhog Day

Ever since Syriza's capitulation, a fog of silence has descended upon Greece. All that one can hear today, after the dust and noise of earlier years settled, is the steady ticking of the clock of a seemingly unstoppable restructuring process.[55] A Groundhog Day of fiscal tightening and economic decline has materialized, further deepening the lack of belief in any possible alternatives. If one tries to find something that differentiates the period of Syriza's rule from the previous pro-austerity governments, two interrelated things stand out. On the one hand, Syriza has proven to be more resilient in implementing austerity, even in areas that all previous authorities avoided or miserably failed.[56] Conversely, what is most strikingly absent from this landscape is the sound of the mobilizations, strikes and imaginative attempts needed to counter such a present and future. It is thus no real surprise that the latest compliance reports from the Troika and the ESM speak so favourably about the government.

Ideology operates at a high level of abstraction. Syriza's remaining local and international supporters,[57] for this reason, have conspicuously failed to recognize that Syriza has not only furthered, if not accelerated, austerity, but it has achieved this without encountering any form of resistance whatsoever.[58] This is not to imply, as some have falsely argued, that Syriza was ever in a position to control or even recuperate social mobilizations. The answer is more likely found in the fact that the capitulation of Syriza represented a failure that was added on top of previous failures, most significantly those born out of the inability of the social movements of 2010–12 to overcome their contradictions

and the authoritarian invariance of government policy. It
is safe to say that many of those who participated in those
mobilizations had already come to see them as hopeless *before*
they ended up voting for Syriza. In any case, the Syriza government has done its best to be added to the long list of governments
whose only role is to firmly embed the notion that there is no
alternative to the disaster of austerity.

# Epilogue: The Future is Not What It Used to Be

Was there ever a realistic alternative? Could Greece have avoided the destructive austerity of the last eight years? This is perhaps the most important, and therefore difficult, question, the significance of which is not merely related to introspection about the past but weighs heavily on possibilities for the future.

For the Troika and its Greek allies, the answer is a simple no. The official story is that Greece's finances were in a terrible shape, the corruption and inefficiency of the state impenetrable and the possibility of continuing down the same road ludicrous. As I have tried to show in this book, the actual motivations behind the 'rescue plans' had little to do with Greece's weak economic performance and its dysfunctional administration. It was imperative for the stability of the economic system to deal with the imminent collapse of the banking sector (primarily the French and German banks, but in this case the Greek ones too), which was triggered by exposure to toxic derivatives from the u.s. and brought to its knees after the Lehman Brothers bankruptcy. Yet at the same time, the austerity reforms that tailgated this bank protection were premised on the primarily ideological presupposition that the implementation of fiscal consolidation, combined with the drastic depreciation of labour costs, would somehow allow the Greek economy to get back on its feet and improve its performance and competitiveness. The idea was that, although reducing deficits and labour costs would lead to a decline in aggregate demand, this could be compensated for by 'importing' demand through boosted exports.[1] This was, after all, the 'expert' opinion that was consistently offered to explain Germany's sound performance and stability throughout the crisis – an argument that, as a matter of fact, betrays a remarkable reluctance to comprehend the historical circumstances that have determined Germany's economic performance. In any case, it was one that those responsible for managing the crisis were eager to copy.[2]

Greek elites were, from the onset, particularly eager to side with this project, though not exactly for the same reasons. Naturally they were concerned with maintaining bank stability (and profitability[3]), but the general outlook of the Troika's programme also coincided with their own macroeconomic models: lower wages and capital consolidation. But what local Troika enthusiasts failed to recognize, and curiously still refuse to acknowledge, was the fact that in an economy structurally based on state subsidies, imports and tax evasion – illegal for most, legal for the rich – the sort of austerity demanded by the lenders would lead to an unprecedented worsening of conditions that would take its toll on everyone, even those who supported the measures. For the tremendous propaganda mechanism put in place an answer was always readily at hand: any sign of generalized decline can (*and should only*) be explained as a consequence of the half-hearted implementation of the reforms, never as a feature of the project itself. Above all else, those promoting this narrative have stubbornly refused to see, and have consistently demonized anyone who claimed otherwise, that the Troika was never particularly concerned with the predestined failure of the Memorandum agreements to regenerate economic activity. In contrast to the illusions maintained by local elites, the lenders' main concern, after the stability of the German and French banks was ensured, was to neutralize Greece's potential systemic risk,[4] not to revitalize economic activity, especially for a country that produces less than 2 per cent of Eurozone GDP. The project of 'saving the Eurozone' was, contrary to various illusions held by Greek supporters of the restructuring process, never based on some overall bourgeois solidarity. In any case, and from the beginning of this saga, the experience provided by the already devastated economies of the former Eastern bloc made austerity's bureaucrats scorn such concepts as that of a 'humanitarian crisis', opting instead to point towards a 'happier' future that would see the Greek economy potentially compete with its Balkan neighbours. If there was ever any 'plan' to revitalize the Greek economy, that would only occur through massive capital consolidation and the reduction of labour costs to the extent of making the economy 'competitive' vis-à-vis the neighbouring Balkan states, not vis-a-vis the rest of Eurozone.

This one-way-street presentation of austerity was, of course, not shared by everyone. But what did those opposed to the restructuring process offer as an alternative to this course? To start with, one has to be clear not to present those who rejected austerity as a monolithic bloc. The economic devastation and drastic breakdown of existing consensus-producing mechanisms generated, as I have described in this book, a wide range of reactions. Retrospectively, one could be permitted to draw a dividing line between those who opposed the restructuring process in the hope of restoring previous conditions and those who, forced by the circumstances and an understanding of the situation, whether tacit or not, questioned the very framework within which 'problems' and 'solutions' were being proposed.

Syriza remains the parliamentary expression par excellence of the first category. From their unsubstantiated pre-election promise to 'tear up' the Memorandum agreements and end austerity, all the way to the government's 'negotiations' with the lenders, Syriza's exclamations never moved beyond the horizon of returning from a horrible present to a glorified past. Whether their programme was Keynesian, social democratic or foolishly utopian was entirely insignificant. What did matter, and what seems to have mobilized people in their support, was a vague promise to return to a mythical moment in time when Greece was sovereign, when the state could (through job creation, investments or the favourable treatment of parts of private capital) maintain economic stability and record 'growth', when the existence of clientelist networks and social alliances provided, despite the absence of social justice, a certain social coherence. This glued together the abstract 'end of austerity' with Syriza's very real favourable treatment of the most privileged public employees, the collaboration with the right-wing ANEL, the various gifts to wealthy businessmen and shipping tycoons, and the patriotic credentials. Above all, it was Syriza's vision of what Greece should look like post-austerity that revealed that its happy future was a relic of the past: restored wages and pensions, a sustainable debt, a banking sector generously giving out loans, a heroic exit to the markets, an effective administration that invites foreign investment and promotes competitiveness – and all that inside the Eurozone. In other words, it was a vision of Greek society as it was, or rather as it saw itself, just before the crisis.

Syriza was not, of course, alone in seeing the restructuring process as a hiccup that had upset what should have been the uninterrupted forward march of pre-existing relations. From their own perspective, a wide range of professional categories, middle-class businessmen and petty bourgeois farmers, to name a few significant categories of Greece's class composition, also put their faith in the possibility of 'ejecting' austerity from their historical reality, even if, and sometimes especially when, that meant that others would pay the price. This is, to be fair, an expected reaction to the sudden and dramatic deterioration of living conditions and the disintegration of social cohesion. But the problem with this vision was not only that it aimed at restoring an already flawed and exploitative society; principally, the problem was that it ignored, much as the Troika pretended to do, the elephant in the room: the very severe crisis of capitalism that had destroyed the foundations upon which the 'growth' and 'prosperity' of past decades had been based. To further clarify, the anti-austerity mobilizations and political programmes that understood stopping the restructuring process as a means of revitalizing pre-existing conditions misinterpreted the nature of the capitalist crisis itself. The perception of the reforms imposed by the Troika as some sort of externally imposed humiliation on the nation or a selective punishment allowed this vision to mystify both the rationale underlying austerity and the possible responses to it.

When these pipe dreams were crushed under the unhinged determination of combined capitalist interests and a reality check forced by the continuation of the global crisis, the previous 'enemies' of the restructuring process (such as Syriza) became, on the spur of the moment, its most effective advocates. But can one really be surprised when those who were eventually selected to oppose austerity based their arguments on the potential for change on Eurogroup meetings, IMF reports or some sort of negotiation about the decimal amount of primary surpluses? What sort of outlook on the world does the belief in these performative spectacles betray, and in what universe could these be the key to putting an end to the deterioration of people's lives?

Fortunately, many of those who participated in the mobilizations never needed the final capitulation of Syriza to discard such illusions. Some had already understood, for example, that an economic restructuring of such devastating consequences can only be rendered unworkable if it is met by a sustained non-payment mobilization at numerous levels. Some were also aware that the idea of austerity as a national humiliation was nothing but an attempt to hide its class character and promote a unifying pseudo-solution through parliamentary means. Above all, quite a few had realized that the victims of austerity do not share the same interests as those who are imposing it.

This refusal to accept the framework within which the discourse around austerity was played out represented, in its full potential, the only possible 'alternative' to the crisis and its management – and this 'alternative' made its appearance, albeit marginally, only during the social movement that opposed the reforms. It was visible when people refused the habitual mediation of politicians, trade unions and mass media and tried to organize themselves and their everyday lives in such a way as to make these institutions obsolete. It arose when people mobilized to refuse collectively the payment of electricity bills, dramatically increased public transport fees or highway tolls, thereby rejecting in practice the notion that the further deterioration of their living conditions was an acceptable sacrifice for a government wishing to appease its lenders. It gained momentum when healthcare workers denied the reality of the collapse of the health system and set up structures that not only tended to those in dire need but produced profound critiques of the commodification of health care. It existed in all those beautiful moments of rupture when people ignored the fear propagandists of all colours and declared that, contrary to their apocalyptic scenarios, the collapse was *already* here and had taken too great a toll.

If these glimpses of a world beyond the normality of capitalist austerity failed to multiply, the reasons should not be sought in their supposedly unrealistic character, for it is precisely the defence of realism that has justified the management of the crisis, the restructuring, the illusory belief that holding one's breath and hoping for the storm to pass is the best strategy, all the while people's lives are irreversibly destroyed. The failure of such subversion to generalize was also not the result of the unleashing of state repression, though this was an undeniable reality; these radical gestures took place in a social field beyond the immediate reach of the police.[5] If these instances remained scattered in the time and space of the social movement, their inability to expand needs to be confronted on its material basis: the difficulty of finding and defending common interests in a world whose perpetuation is based on generalized separation, especially when this division is not merely the result of some external imposition, but is adopted and reproduced by those who would have much to gain from its disappearance. Even when social movements break the continuity of normality, the scope of confrontation is not confined to a clear and opposing enemy. It includes a confrontation with people's own past activity, the crystallized form of our lives *within* capitalist relations, which have permeated and commodified our understanding of the world. The celebrated individual of modernity, the one that developments of the last thirty years have reduced to a 'minimal self', not only lives in isolation but appears to thrive in it. Is there another way to explain why the succession of monologues featured in the Syntagma Square occupation was celebrated as some kind of breakthrough? And yet, it is never only our isolation that we bring with us in social struggles: it is also our *sociality*, one torn between defending its existing and limited coordinates and a desire to be rediscovered outside this framework. To the extent that subversion starts to make practical and material sense, possibilities expand. Or, as a slogan in the streets of Athens put it, 'barricades open up paths'.

Nonetheless, it remains crucial to emphasize that the failure to stop the restructuring process can in no way be explained simply by looking inside Greece, another point that this book has tried to demonstrate. Greece's position within the international division of the capitalist economy was, and is even more today, one of relative isolation. The opening-up of borders to allow capital in- and outflows and the movement of documented labour did not and could not bring about some proletarian unification,

while the calls of an insignificant Left for solidarity between
the 'people of Europe' or at least of 'the South' were cancelled
out by the same Left's unashamed insistence on national narratives
of all types. Contrary to these abstractions, the only 'solidarity'
that has so far made its way across borders is, ironically, the
national narrative, an approach that condemns all those deprived
of any control over their lives – and know it – to the consequences
of the economic crisis.

The era of 'limitless' credit expansion came to an end in 2008.
Although this abrupt ending allowed governments and monetary
authorities to reconfigure the direction of economic policies
towards austerity, this response failed to address the essence
of the crisis itself: the decline in profitability.[6] Contrary to pronouncements about the end of the economic slump and signs of
growth, which have been repeated almost every year since 2009,
most available data points to the exact opposite: at best, sluggish
growth, minimal investments (if any) and stagnant profitability.
And all this despite mild or harsh austerity and despite the use
of 'unorthodox' and monetary tools that were unthinkable until
a few years back. All the while, the decline continues to affect
people's lives and to elicit reactions of various forms. But today's
predicament, itself a product of the failure of previous social
movements, has unfortunately shown that responses to the
continuing crisis seem to have lost their emancipatory potentials
and have reverted to a reactionary backlash that takes the
meaning of national politics to its inevitable conclusion.[7]

The process of accelerating the interlinkage of the global
economy ('globalization') did not generate a globalization of
struggles, as some had wished. But it was not, at the same
time, a purely positive process for capitalist accumulation.
The very expansion of the financial form of capitalism and
the interconnectedness it produced also meant that a collapse
in one sector (in the most recent case, a small section of real

estate in the u.s.) immediately spread across the global economy, thereby threatening its whole structure. Those in almost unquestioned charge of managing capitalist affairs for the last thirty years proceeded from a shared ideological perspective and chose a mix of austerity for the poor and, to borrow Robert Brenner's phrase, 'asset Keynesianism' for the rich. But even though this produced a certain 'stability', a term that today signifies nothing more than the averting of total collapse, capitalist social relations do not simply depend on avoiding catastrophe or ensuring that those close to ruling elites will survive financial difficulties. It requires, above all else, that the labour-capital relation be configured in such a way as to generate increased profits (value). When this straightforward relationship is disrupted, no amount of unconventional money creation and/or diminished labour costs will, in itself, rebalance the equation.

The failure of this reconfiguration has, however, created a backlash from certain sectors of the capitalist class, who remain justifiably unsatisfied with the current stagnation/deflation. This fact, combined with the chronic dissatisfaction of proletarians who have had to bear the burden of the crisis, has generated a new dynamic that could herald a paradigm shift for the global capitalist economy. The result of the UK referendum in favour of Brexit and, most crucially, the election of Donald Trump in the u.s. have opened up the prospect of a reversal of globalization and a return of protectionism. In its essence, this tendency seeks to 're-nationalize' the main economic coordinates, by re-establishing the state mechanism as the key mediation protecting capitalist interests from the turbulence of the global market and its national citizens from its effects.

Many have tried to explain this development as a resurgence of the reactionary Right, something that the sensibilities of its main proponents (such as Trump) seem to justify. But what this account misses entirely is that the official Left, with its anti-globalization slogans, its call for 'national reconstruction' and its promise to prioritize the well-being of its national working class,[8] approaches the issue from a similar angle. In any case, the future realization of such a fundamental shift away from the dominant mode of capitalist expansion does not, in itself, depend on the expressed political orientation of those in charge. Above all, it depends on the economic ability of the interested countries to survive such a disturbance and reorientation, a veritable shock that only countries like the u.s., with its international hegemonic role and its vast internal market, or perhaps China might be able to withstand, leaving the rest to compete ruthlessly for a better position within this new international division.

Whether the national/protectionist tendency will actually gain momentum and become a reality is, like every prediction, highly questionable. But it remains an unfortunate characteristic of our historical period that this direction appears as the only 'challenge' to the existing management model of the continuing crisis, a realization that allows one to return to the main subject of this book for a final observation: if Greece is paying the harsh price of austerity, it is not because of a reckless spending past; it is paying the price of capitalism's present miserable state, whose gridlock offers no chance of improvement in the foreseeable future.

# References

## Introduction

1    International Monetary Fund, 'Greece: Preliminary Debt Sustainability Analysis: Updated Estimates and Further Considerations', www.imf.org, May 2016.

2    In 2005 there were 250,000 real estate sales in Athens alone. In 2014 the number of sales had fallen to 3,600. The inability to sell, coupled with the unbearable property tax, has led to a more than 56 per cent decline in accepting property inheritance only in the last three years – all this in a country that has the highest percentage of home ownership (87 per cent) in the EU.

3    Although schematic, the mentioned distinction roughly separates liberal/neoliberal from left-wing analyses of the Greek crisis. In the category of focusing too much on Greece's internal problems, one finds the recent books of Yannis Palaiologos, *The 13th Labour of Hercules: Inside the Greek Crisis* (London, 2014) and James Angelos, *The Full Catastrophe: Inside the Greek Crisis* (London, 2015). On the opposite side, one finds Yanis Varoufakis's *And the Weak Suffer What They Must: Europe, Austerity and the Threat to Global Stability* (London, 2016). In a special category of its own, ex-Finance Minister George Papaconstantinou's *Game Over: The Inside Story of the Greek Crisis* (CreateSpace, 2016) is a good example of the incredible ideological nonsense that one who held such a crucial post pretends to believe in.

## 1 A Thing of the Past

1    Henry C. K. Liu, 'U.S. Dollar Hegemony Has Got to Go', *Asia Times*, www.atimes.com, 11 April 2002.

2    ELAS (Greek Popular Liberation Army) was the military wing of EAM (National Liberation Front), an organization led by KKE (Communist Party of Greece). The pro-Soviet KKE had created EAM in accordance with the Popular Front strategy that sought alliances with progressive and patriotic bourgeois elements. It was by far the

most organized and numerically significant guerrilla army during the occupation of Greece. According to some estimates, EAM had around 1 million members, while ELAS claimed around 300,000 soldiers and supporters at a time when the total population of Greece was approximately 6.7 million. For reasons of comparison, the next-largest resistance group of the Right (EDES) numbered around 10,000 members and supporters.

3   Those who belonged to or were associated with the Left were immediately deemed 'communist'. At the time, being a 'communist' was synonymous with being a spy, which meant being excluded from the 'national community'. One may have mistakenly assumed that the collaborators of the Nazis would merit exclusion from the 'national community', but shifting geopolitical relations did not allow for such a narrative, leaving the popular demand to punish collaborators unanswered. For details, see Mark Mazower, ed., *After the War Was Over* (Princeton, NJ, 2000), especially Eleni Haidia, 'The Punishment of Collaborators in Northern Greece, 1945–1946', pp. 42–61.

4   All state employees were forced to sign such declarations. Those who did not were summarily fired, further ensuring that the state mechanism was dominated by the right wing for the next decades. At the same time, in one of the typical examples of Stalinist irrationality and discipline, KKE instructed its members to refuse to sign these declarations, transforming the issue into one of pride and honour. In the same way that the Right considered those not signing as 'traitors', KKE used the same terminology for those who did. In reality, and contrary to the Party's instructions, it seems that a large number of political prisoners did sign them, quite often under pressure from their families.

5   Until the 1960s the agricultural sector in Greece contributed 50 per cent of GDP and 30 per cent of employment.

6   From 1956 to 1966, 679,000 Greeks migrated to Europe (mostly Belgium and Germany), half a million of them during the second half of this period (1961–6). It has already been mentioned how migration from the south to the north contributed to the productive capacity of European capitalism. Here we see how this was not only beneficial for the receiving countries of migrant labour, but for the countries of origin too as it allowed them to 'export' their social conflicts.

7   The Fiscal Committee of the Central Bank was created for precisely that reason. Its structure clearly indicated the level of dependence of the Greek economy on foreign aid, with two foreign experts always appointed at its head. The Fiscal Committee was abolished in 1981 in one of Andreas Papandreou's many symbolic gestures.

8   In every minor or major social, political or economic disturbance, the quest for gold reached fever pitch. That was the case, for

example, with the 1963 elections and the instability they produced, forcing the Central Bank to suggest getting out of the gold trade. The government rejected this, forcing the Central Bank to experience serious problems with its gold reserves in 1965.

9    In Greece, as elsewhere, a rise in the industrial working class mirrored a decrease of the agricultural population. As with other countries of the European south, the persistence of a large agricultural sector was a constant headache for those who sought to modernize the country. In any case, however, and despite constant attempts, Greece never became an industrial country. The industrial workforce never exceeded 20 per cent of the total workforce, while its contribution to GDP was, at its highest moment in 1981, at 30 per cent.

10   The liberalization was not only a demand of the marginalized Left. The post-civil war landscape was increasingly characterized by explosive contradictions that were becoming veritable obstacles to capitalist development itself. As Elefantis remarked, 'For two whole decades, and while Sygrou Avenue was getting occupied by car dealerships, the state obstructed the circulation of the car-commodity by demanding from consumers a "certificate of political beliefs" in exchange for a drivers' license. It thus excluded, on extra-economic and purely political grounds, a whole category of consumers.' Angelos Elefantis, *In the Constellation of Populism* (Athens, 1991), p. 67.

11   In 1961 there were sixty recorded strikes, corresponding to 157,000 lost hours. In 1964 the number increased to 227 strikes, equivalent to 1,124,000 hours of lost work. By 1966, 196 strikes resulted in 1,342,000 lost work hours.

12   For the first time since the end of the war, the period between 1962 and 1967 saw real wages surpassing productivity increases.

13   The coup d'état was organized and carried out by a group of army colonels who had been trained by U.S. intelligence officers and were, as employees of the Minister of Interior, paid directly by the U.S. embassy. Even if no tangible evidence of U.S. involvement in the planning and execution of the coup can be provided, there is no doubt that the U.S. government immediately recognized and supported the junta as an important anti-communist ally in Eastern Europe. Immediately after the coup's success, for example, Senator Lee Metcalf criticized the Johnson Administration for providing aid to a 'military regime of collaborators and Nazi sympathizers'.

14   In 1971 alone the junta received more than $250 million in loans. In the same year, total expenditure for interest payments reached 12.4 per cent of GDP, compared to 7.8 per cent in 1966.

15   Bank credits to construction and housing fell by 38 per cent. The dire situation was further worsened by a total fall in investments from the private sector (–20 per cent), the state sector (–27.7 per cent), industrial production (–31 per cent) and productivity (–15 per cent).

16  Contrary to the post-dictatorship myth (promoted by parts of the Left as well), the uprising in the Polytechnic in November 1973 was not a conflict between peaceful students and violent military/police personnel. The mobilization of the army units was itself the direct consequence of the inability of the police to manage the violence of those in the streets, who had, among other things, burned down the police headquarters. The classic work that dispels those myths and gives a breathtaking account of those days remains Stergios Katsaros, Εγώ ο προβοκάτορας, ο τρομοκράτης ['I, the Provocateur, the Terrorist'] (Athens, 2008).

17  The end of the dictatorship saw a symbolic repetition of the end of the Second World War. In the same way that the Greek Left bore the burden and high cost of resistance to the Nazi occupation but was swiftly forced to abandon any dreams of gaining power in 1944, the Greek Right, in self-imposed exile during the Junta, was eager (and eventually successful) in ensuring that an empowered Left would not rise to the opportunity in 1974.

18  See Panos Loukakos, 'Chronicle of the First Days After the Junta', *Nea Estia*, CLXXV/1862 (June 2014), p. 379.

19  Marking a radical shift from the policies of the 1950s and '60s, Zolotas's 1975 annual 'Report of the Central Bank of Greece' declared aggregate demand as the key indicator of economic performance and the basis for any hope for an increase in the productive capacity. 'If the real income of workers falls, aggregate demand also falls and in this way production is reduced. There are, therefore, not only social reasons, but also economic ones, which testify for the need to maintain the purchasing power of the worker's income.' Xenophon Zolotas, *Our Economic Problem*, Bank of Greece (Athens, 1975).

20  Some years later, the results of the suppression of autonomous workplace organizations would be celebrated in another conference of the Greek Industrialists' Union (ΣΕΒ): 'The old spontaneity which characterized the 1974–1977 period tends to be replaced by processes that allow for the more permanent and more responsible presence of unionists in the everyday requirements of the enterprise.' Both quotes are found in Ntantis-Lazaros Doukakis, 'Work Relations and the Form of the Wage Relation during the Post-war Industrialization and Crisis', *Greek Review of Social Research*, no. 59 (1985), pp. 3–40.

21  Labour Minister K. Laskaris's statement in 1976 was indicative: 'We will not allow for the existence of the class struggle', using ambiguity to imply both that the notion of the 'class struggle' was not accepted as a category in a liberal society while also hinting at its criminalization.

## 2 The Monetarist Transformation

1   Tracing the historical emergence of the term 'neoliberalism' or locating the theoretical projections of its advocates is, though possible, somehow misleading. There is no purity of theoretical constructs, in the same way that the transmission mechanisms that create economic policy out of theoretical 'manuals' are rather elusive. On top of all that, the term 'neoliberalism' has acquired, especially for the Left, an almost 'magical' essence, virtually indistinguishable from the historical development of capitalism per se. This confusion and mystification demands that the term be, at least, used within inverted commas.

2   Put simply, monetarism views the supply of money (i.e. the total amount of currency in circulation and easily accessible deposits) and not aggregate demand as the primary determinant of economic activity and the basis of economic policy. Inflation, for example, is caused by the fact that *too much* money is chasing *too few* goods. Controlling the quantity of money can bring it in line with the growth rate of production.

3   One example is the famous Philip's Curve, a model equation that projects a historically inverse relationship between inflation and unemployment.

4   Another immediate consequence was a destabilization of the international financial system, hitting developing countries that had borrowed heavily, plunging them into a debt spiral. To manage this predicament, institutions such as the IMF, in its newly acquired role as international monetary cop, stepped in and started enforcing its policies of austerity in exchange for bail-outs.

5   Raising interest rates promotes the withdrawing of money from circulation and thus, according to monetarist orthodoxy, the reduction of inflation.

6   Most investments take place through loans. When interest rates are high, capitalists are forced to pay back more for their loans, something that acts as a disincentive for investments.

7   For Keynesians, the 'natural rate' was around 3–4 per cent. Monetarists managed to double that. As Norfield notes, 'In the UK in the 1960s, an unemployment figure of 500,000 was considered to be a disgrace to the government in power; by the late 1970s, getting unemployment below a million was seen as a result . . . Getting UK unemployment below two million is seen as progress today!' Tony Norfield, *The City: London and the Global Power of Finance* (London, 2016), p. 53, footnote p. 237.

8   In what was celebrated as Reagan's first show of force in 1980, the massive strike of 13,000 air-traffic controllers organized around the PATCO union was swiftly crushed when the newly elected president

immediately fired 11,345 of them, banning them from federal service for life. The official excuse was that their strike violated a 1947 federal law that forbids government employees from striking, but the propaganda used to justify this unprecedented anti-strike repression was that the air-traffic controllers were part of a 'workers' aristocracy' who led wealthy lives at the expense of taxpayers.

9   Employment in public corporations fell from 1,867,000 in 1981, to 599,000 in 1991 and 379,000 in 2002. Philip Arestis and Malcolm Sawyer, 'The Neoliberal Experience of the United Kingdom', in *Neoliberalism: A Critical Reader*, ed. Alfredo Saad-Filho and Deborah Johnston (London, 2005), p. 205.

10  According to monetarist orthodoxy, 'the stable value of money is to be maintained at all cost, except for speculative growth, which it translated to mean ever-rising share prices. Rising share prices, unlike rising wages, are not viewed as inflation, a rationale hard to understand.' Henry C. K. Liu, 'The Lessons of the u.s. Experience', *Asia Times*, www.atimes.com, 21 December 2002.

11  For example, various studies have shown that precarious and part-time labour conditions fail, in the long run, to reconfigure the capital/labour relation in a manner that increases capital returns. See, for example, D. W. Jorgenson, M. S. Ho and K. J. Stiroh, 'A Retrospective Look at the u.s. Productivity Growth Resurgence', *Journal of Economic Perspectives*, xxii/1 (2008), pp. 3–24; P. Auer, J. Berg and I. Coulibaly, 'Is a Stable Workforce Good for Productivity?', *International Labour Review*, cxliv/3 (2005), pp. 319–43; Y. Kılıçaslan and E. Taymaz, 'Labor Market Institutions and Industrial Performance: An Evolutionary Study', *Journal of Evolutionary Economics*, xviii (2008), pp. 477–92; E. Toledo, 'The Crisis of the Maquiladora Model in Mexico', *Work and Occupations*, xxxiv/4 (2007), pp. 349–429.

12  This was a change that needs to be seen as a quantitative (and not qualitative) expansion of earlier moves. See Norfield, *The City: London and the Global Power of Finance*.

13  But, crucially, not value. The finance sector should be understood as the mechanism for the allocation and distribution of surplus value created in the production process. See Duncan K. Foley, 'Rethinking Financial Capitalism and the "Information" Economy', *Review of Radical Political Economics*, xlv/3 (2013), pp. 257–68.

14  It was formalized through the 1982 Garn-St Germain Act and the 1987 Financial Institutions Reform and Recovery Act.

15  The structure of the banking system in the u.s., the Glass-Steagall Act of 1933 and the specific arrangement of Bretton Woods had resulted in a situation where 'many u.s. banks did not even play much of a role in the *national* banking system, let alone internationally'. Norfield, *The City: London and the Global Power of Finance*, p. 40.

16  'Any large-scale investment programme necessary to develop export industries would result in an initial surge in imports of raw materials and other commodities necessary to set up production. This would lead to a sharp rise in the outflow of u.s. dollars to pay for them until production was up and running and the dollar revenues from export sales began to flow in. With limited dollar reserves any government attempting to promote such an investment programme would soon find itself with a serious currency crisis on its hands.' 'Return of the Crisis, Part ii: The Nature and Significance of the Crisis', *Aufheben*, no. 19 (2011), p. 17, available at http://libcom.org, accessed 10 February 2018.

17  Overcapacity led to slower demand, forcing many developing economies to crumble under their inability to repay their dollar-denominated and high interest rate debt. In response, imf and World Bank-led restructuring programmes were imposed on them with very harsh austerity measures attached.

18  It was called the 'Snake in the Tunnel' due to its graphic depiction. The exchange rate turbulence was hindering inter-European trade and the free movement of capital. The reason for this was rather simple: if credit were given in the currency of the creditor, the borrower could suffer the effects of the creditor's currencies' devaluation and thus be forced to pay back more in the end. If the credit was given in the currency of the borrower, the creditor had no idea what he would get paid in the end. For this reason, before the euro, foreign investors demanded insurance premiums to offset the risk of depreciation. The introduction of the euro abolished such 'hindrances'.

19  Authors as different in perspective as Yanis Varoufakis (*And the Weak Suffer What They Must: Europe, Austerity and the Threat to Global Stability*, London, 2016 and Hans-Werner Sinn (*The Euro Trap*, Oxford, 2014) suggest that Mitterrand's Finance Minister Jacques Delors convinced him to proceed with austerity merely as a strategic choice that would eventually allow France not only to resume a 'socialist' agenda, but to convince Germany to adopt one too. For what it's worth, today's Syriza government also claims occasionally that its capitulation to austerity is part of a carefully thought-out strategy.

20  Guy Abeille, 'A l'origine du déficit à 3 per cent du pib, une invention 100 per cent . . . française', *La Tribune*, www.latribune.fr, 1 October 2010.

21  The Single European Act was a significant revision of the semi-Keynesian-influenced Rome Treaty of 1957, which included many anachronistic restrictions on finance and the free movement of capital.

22  Unification had produced an inflationary pressure on the German economy. That was mainly due to the overvaluation of the

East German Mark, which, to the detriment of the Bundesbank, was seen as the only way to put a stop to the mass migration of workers from the East to the West (and companies from the West to the East).

23  It was only through mechanisms designed to guarantee the stability of the common currency that Germany would be convinced to abandon the Deutsch Mark. Moreover, the most important clauses (on debt and deficit) mirrored not simply the exact predicament of the German economy at the time, but its ideal and primary aim.

24  Of course such a resource-transferring mechanism aiming at balancing out unequal economic development exists *within* countries such as Germany (from the West to the East) or Italy (from the North to the South). For Varoufakis, the implementation of such a mechanism at Eurozone level is his battle cry: see Varoufakis, *And the Weak Suffer What They Must.*

25  In the context of the global market, when a country such as Germany raises its interest rates, it attracts capital that is fleeing from places with lower rates or less stable currencies. One of the weapons that national central banks have to counteract currency depreciation caused by capital flight is to spend their foreign reserves to prop up their own currency.

26  David Marsh, *The Euro: The Battle for the New Global Currency* (London, 2011), p. 191.

27  In 1991 Italy's budget deficit was an incredible 11.4 per cent, while its debt-to-GDP ratio was more than 100 per cent. By 1998, the convergence reference date for the EMU, Italy's public debt was almost double what Maastricht allowed (118.1 per cent of GDP), though its deficit had fallen to 2.5 per cent; European Monetary Institute, *Convergence Report: Report Required by Article 109j of the Treaty Establishing the European Community*, March 1998, www.ecb.europa.eu, p. 19.

28  Between the collapse of Bretton Woods (1971) and the introduction of the EMU (1999), the Italian lira had been devalued 13 times (and revalued only once).

29  In terms of the public debt limit (60 per cent of GDP), only Finland, France and the UK were eligible (though the UK was not even interested in joining the EMU). Even Germany had a debt ratio slightly above the Maastricht criteria (61.3 per cent), as the EU had forced them to include the re-unification obligations in the government debt. Countries such as Ireland, Spain and Portugal were at 66.3 per cent, 68.8 per cent and 62 per cent, respectively, whereas Italy (121.6 per cent) and Greece (108.7 per cent) were not even close. Deficit numbers were in slightly better shape (only Greece was beyond the 3 per cent threshold, at 4 per cent), with most countries slightly beyond 2 per cent.

30  Quoted in Marsh, *The Euro: The Battle for the New Global Currency*, p. 200.

## 3 A Green Sun

1   Georgios Papandreou was first appointed Prime Minister of Greece in May 1944, in a pre-emptive attempt by King George II and the British to mediate the simmering conflicts in Greece. His failure to do so led to his resignation shortly after the Nazi withdrawal. For the next decade, he served in various governmental positions until finally creating his own centrist party in 1961. Cashing in on the anti-democratic tradition of conservative forces and their stranglehold on power, Papandreou exploited and expressed the progressive elements of the bourgeoisie, a strategy that saw him re-elected prime minister for the second time after the elections of 1963. The combined pressure from the palace and extreme right-wing elements in key army positions, eventually culminating in losing a vote of confidence led by Konstantinos Mitsotakis, forced him to dismiss his government in 1965. Georgios Papandreou's funeral in 1968 (the second year of the dictatorship) became the rallying point for a massive pro-democratic demonstration.

2   In an interesting historical note, Andreas Papandreou was one of the representatives of the Greek government during the Bretton Woods Conference in 1944.

3   The parliamentary Left was divided between the pro-Soviet KKE and the anaemic, Eurocommunist KKE ES. The KKE drew (and continues to draw) its main support from its historical tradition, a fact that unavoidably leads it to be permanently stuck in the past, whereas the KKE ES was characterized by an uneasy mix of structuralist Marxism and pro-European social democracy. Even so, the combined electoral power of the Left never surpassed 14–15 per cent – until, that is, the electoral victory of Syriza in 2015.

4   Lest we forget, the slogan that the neo-Nazi Golden Dawn screams today ('Greece belongs to the Greeks') was first used by Andreas Papandreou, in whose day the slogan had an anti-imperialist flavour. Today it is xenophobic. In either case, however, the goal is the same: a process of unification on the basis of the national community.

5   Most of the companies that received such generous gifts in the 1980s would remain afloat (and uncompetitive) until the early 1990s, when Mitsotakis's New Democracy government embarked on a largely unsuccessful programme to privatize them.

6   Declaration of the Principles of PASOK, 1981.

7   For an introduction to the historical background of this social relation, one should check the excellent essay of Panagiotis Kondylis, 'Origins of the Decadence of Modern Greece',

Introduction to *The Decline of Bourgeois Thought- and Life-forms: The Liberal Modern and the Mass-democratic Post-modern* (Athens, 1991).

8   Exactly like Reagan's and Thatcher's arguments, Papandreou's arguments at the time made reference to 'worker aristocracies': 'Strikes and irrational sectoral demands are consistently brought forward by workers or public-sector unions who happen to be, as a rule, privileged . . . This is the biggest obstacle to the reconfiguration of our economy and the increase of productivity.' Quoted in G. Marinos, 'There is a communication problem', *Oikonomikos Tahidromos* [Economic Courier], no. 22 (June 1983), p. 4 [Greek].

9   As Papandreou famously stated at the time, '[N]o policy is pro-worker if it does not guarantee productivity increases and the conditions for growth.' Speech at the Thessaloniki International Exhibition (ΔΕΘ), September 1982.

10  In 1983 PASOK brought forward a new law, the title of which referred to the 'socialization of enterprises'. Though it was claimed to be a law that empowered the position of workers within companies, a particular section (Article 4) became a source of major controversy. This article stated that for a strike to take place in the public sector, it would have to be voted for by a majority of workers who belonged to the trade union, and not a majority of those who attended the assembly (in which only a small part ever participated). Effectively, this made it particularly difficult to attain a majority for a legal strike.

11  Seventy per cent of this precarious and temporary work was performed by women. Ntantis-Lazaros Doukakis, 'Work Relations and the Form of the Wage Relation during the Post-war Industrialization and Crisis', *Greek Review of Social Research*, no. 59 (1985), pp. 3–40 [Greek].

12  *Oikonomikos Tahidromos*, 4 February 1982 [Greek].

13  Though private capital representatives avoided admitting this at all costs, the effects of EU membership and the international crisis were the key factors that explained the loss of competitiveness. For example, this argument is found constantly in all the OECD's Economic Surveys on Greece throughout the period 1983 to 1989.

14  The rationale behind this is worth quoting: 'The wages of workers, which determine to a large extent the cost of production, are from a certain point of view lower in relation to wages in Europe and North America, but labour productivity is also lower, which means that, despite lower wages, our products are in fact more expensive when viewed in terms of quality.' Kostas Simitis interview, *Oikonomikos Tahidromos*, 24 October 1985. Interestingly, since competitiveness and productivity increases were the order of the day, and PASOK saw itself as the political representative of the working class, it was claimed by both government and employers that tightly connecting

wages and productivity represent the fulfilment of workers' demands. See L. Smailis, 'The Majority of Workers Demand a Connection between Wages and Productivity', *Oikonomikos Tahidromos*, no. 18 (May 1989), pp. 82–7 [Greek].

15 'The economic developments of the last years, and especially of 1985, have shown that the current account payment balance is the main factor limiting the exercise of economic policy', from the 'Yearly Report of the Head of the Bank of Greece' (1985), p. 20 [Greek].

16 Ibid., p. 15.

17 Ibid., p. 23.

18 *Rizospastis* [The Radical], 28 May 1987 [Greek].

19 'It is a midsummer night's dream that the public sector, the way it is today, can take over the responsibilities that belong to the private sector.' Quoted in *Oikonomikos Tahidromos*, 16 January 1986 [Greek].

20 For some workers it was cut altogether, for others it was readjusted to signify foregone inflation rates rather than expected ones.

21 OECD, *Economic Survey of Greece, 1986/1987* (Paris, 1987), pp. 14, 15, 22. In terms of state-led investment, public funding of private investments went from 12 billion drachmas in 1986 to 36.5 billion in 1988.

22 From 527,000 in 1981, public sector employees had reached 570,000 in 1985.

23 The low-quality service provided by many public sectors makes this abstraction easier to swallow, though there is no obvious connection between the two.

24 OECD, *Economic Survey of Greece, 1989/1990* (Paris, 1990), p. 38.

25 'Yearly Report of the Head of the Bank of Greece' (1985), p. 18.

26 *Eleftherotypia* [Press Freedom], 10 July 1986 [Greek].

27 In this period, the government had voted for the liberalization of the media frequencies and their opening up to private interests. This led to a bitter competition to gain access to these outlets, a conflict overshadowed by the state and its desire to ensure that privately owned media would remain government-friendly.

28 In his annual report of 1989, Chalikias stated, 'The main characteristic of the direction of the economy in 1989 is the reversal of the progress that was observed after the implementation of the "stabilization programme" of 1985–1987 . . . due to the further increase of public deficit and debt . . . The worsening of the economic imbalances is, by far, a consequence of the expansive fiscal policy that was implemented from 1988 onwards. More specifically, it was inevitable that constant increase in public spending, widened tax evasion, tax gifts and the rapid rise in real wages would lead the economy to overheat and, through that, would increase inflationary pressures and public deficit.' 'Yearly Report of the Head of the Bank of Greece' (1989), p. 14.

29  PASOK also had its share in police brutality. In 1985, for example, during riots in the 'infamous' Exarchia area, a policeman had shot and killed a fifteen-year-old demonstrator in the back of the head.

30  In the end, only eleven of the 64 firms that were meant to be privatized were actually sold.

31  'Yearly Report of the Head of the Bank of Greece' (1994), p. 16.

32  Though neoliberal in theory, New Democracy was, of course, more tightly bound by clientelist relations as their political and electoral careers depended heavily on their ability to replace PASOK's guard with their own.

33  The role of the bloody conflict in Yugoslavia in producing a remarkable nationalist unification in Greece has, unfortunately, received little attention. This was a moment when different sides of the political spectrum practically joined forces, revealing embarrassingly common sensitivities between the ultra-conservative Church, neo-Nazis and the Left. For the Left, support for Milošević was a proud manifestation (and relic) of its anti-imperialist/anti-U.S. credentials. For the Church, it represented a moment of religious solidarity towards the Orthodox Serbs (whose existence as 'orthodox' no one even knew prior to the war). Nationalist/neo-Nazi thugs, on the other hand, were attracted by the presentation of the conflict (by nationalist Serbs) as a revival of a battleground against Turks and Muslims. Though the Left and the Church could only offer financial, political and diplomatic support to the nationalist Serbs, neo-Nazis went a step further when some of their members participated as mercenaries in ethnic-cleansing paramilitary Serbian groups. To understand the extent to which the identification with Serbia was unquestioned in Greek society, one only needs to know that, upon returning, some of these Nazis proudly admitted their participation in the Srebrenica massacre, without this revelation causing any particular uproar (until late 2017, when a prosecutor decided to reopen the case).

34  In 1992 the recorded ratio was at 89.0 per cent. Ralph C. Bryant, Nicholas C. Garganas and George S. Tavlas, eds, *Greece's Economic Performance and Prospects*, Bank of Greece/Brooklings Institution (Athens, 2001).

35  It would take another eleven full years before New Democracy got another chance to see the inside of a government cabinet.

36  This section owes much to the brilliant paper of Giannis Balabanidis, '"For a Strong Society, for a Strong Greece": A Critical Overview of the Modernizing Project (1996–2004), 'Politics and Ideology' (May 2007) [Greek], Master's thesis, University of Panteion.

37  This statement is true if one takes the two and a half years that Simitis acted as finance minister, as well as his almost nine years as prime minister (1995–2004).

38  'In the case of Greece, we are faced with a typical example of the weaknesses of the model of growth dependency, in the framework of which there was no adoption of any policies that would allow the national productive forces to progressively replace foreign capital in their role of defining factors of industrialisation . . . Faced with this reality, two elements obtain strategic importance: the role of the State and that of technology. Technology because it consists of the basis through which industry can support its transition to alternative forms of regulation of the accumulation process . . . The issues that lie in the epicentre of social conflicts, the importance of the form of accumulation and of labour relations, of technology, of the manner through which the Greek economy gets integrated in the global market, all these reveal the structural character of the problems. These elements also spell out the field and limits of the activities of the State. But the quest for a new balance demands a new type of relation between State and the economy.' Tasos Giannitsis, *Greece: Industrialization in Crisis* (Athens, 1986), pp. 261–4 (my translation), quoted in Balabanidis, '"For a Strong Society"', p. 24.

39  Similar developments took place throughout Europe, such as the Elia Coalition in Italy, which won the elections in 1996. Their policies were also characterized by the process of realignment towards the Eurozone, privatizations and the adoption of monetarism, visible in the rendering of the Central Bank of Italy 'independent' from the state.

40  Most of these proposals can be found in the works of the main ideologue and intellectual of New Labour, Anthony Giddens, in his *Beyond Left and Right: The Future of Radical Politics* (Cambridge, 1994) and *The Third Way: The Renewal of Social Democracy* (Cambridge, 1998).

41  This point is crucial in framing an understanding that came to be seen as an alternative route to the crisis management of the Troika and the successive Greek governments (and eventually to the 'anti-globalization' sentiments behind Trump and Brexit). This 'alternative' (whether from Syriza or the Left, or from elements of the Right, including the neo-Nazis of Golden Dawn) seeks a return to national sovereignty as the key to unlocking the potential of an economy devastated by foreign rule and Troika commands or, in other words, 'globalization'.

42  Yannis Stournaras, *The Perspective of Modernization in Greece* (Athens, 2002). Stournaras was later appointed finance minister by Antonis Samaras (2012–14), and is currently (June 2018) serving as Governor of the Bank of Greece.

43   It is thus not at all surprising that a significant number of KKE ES supporters found in Simitis a governmental expression of their own beliefs. Their adherence to this 'modernizing' line of thought, lured by a commitment to a rather distorted notion of social justice, was not, as some claim, a moment of betrayal of their left principles or mere 'opportunism'. It was, in fact, a specific continuation of already established beliefs, coloured by the new circumstances imposed by the global transformations of capitalism since the 1970s and, perhaps more specifically for Greece, the collapse of the Soviet Union. A very significant part of this part of the Greek intelligentsia was, for a long time, ready to engage with the modernizing faction of PASOK, and the personal trajectories of many of its members prove this beyond doubt. In contrast to this, Syriza tried to revive itself by opting for the less extreme elements of the anti-globalization movement of the late 1990s and early 2000s.

44   The typical leftist approach which proclaims that 'capital has no fatherland', or that globalization does away with national sovereignty, not only betrays the Left's deeply patriotic ideological constitution. It misinterprets and mystifies the dynamic process of capitalist development. Even in its most extreme forms, the advent of globalization and the coordination of market forces through (selected) global institutions does not abolish or replace the nation-state as the elementary form within which capitalist social relations flourish and develop. It simply reconfigures it in accordance with the historical development of the necessities of capitalist accumulation.

45   The completion of this transformation would be top of the agenda in the Memorandum agreements of the Troika after 2010.

46   The construction industry contributed, in the period between 1995 and 2002, approximately 8.6 per cent of GDP, prompting the ECB to warn of the excessive dependence of the Greek economy on this sector; *Eleftherotypia*, 15 September 2003.

47   This was a process of reconfiguration of the concept of *citizenship* as *exclusion*.

48   Public investments rose at a rate of 9.4 per cent per year, while private ones followed a little bit behind at 7 per cent.

49   Before becoming apologists and dedicated enforcers of harsh austerity policies, Syriza intellectuals were well aware of these obvious configurations. For example, see Georgios Stathakis, 'Economic Liberalism and the Project of Modernization', in *Ideological Currents and Tendencies of Intellectuals in Modern Greece*, 8th Scientific Conference, Panteion University, Sakis Karagiorgas Foundation, Athens, 2002.

50   This ideological crescendo produced a very particular school of thought for journalists and analysts. In their vision, for example,

the anachronistic Left and part of the business world share common interests and fight together against the benevolent forces of modernization. This surreal approach informs many of today's liberal 'critiques' of Syriza's government.

51  A recent example of this ideological belief can be found in Giannis Palaiologos, *The 13th Labour of Hercules: Inside the Greek Crisis* (London, 2014). Interestingly enough, Gianis Varoufakis's own recent book *And the Weak Suffer What They Must: Europe, Austerity and the Threat to Global Stability* (London, 2016), which claims to provide an analysis of the historical background of the recent crisis, entirely ignores this whole period.

52  The example of the 1998 strikes and riots against the educational reforms or the massive mobilizations in 2000 against social insurance reforms were among them.

53  It took seven years of harsh austerity for some to whisper reluctantly that higher wages are actually beneficial for GDP growth, while the secure status of public employees encourages spending, thereby boosting demand. The fact that the genius plan of slashing them right and left would lead to a dramatic fall in demand and the further decline of economic performance still appears to surprise some people.

## 4 'Holy Cow!'

The title of this chapter is taken from Christine Lagarde's reaction upon hearing that Lehman Brothers had gone under. Kim Willsher, 'Christine Lagarde: The Woman Who Would be the World's Banker', *The Guardian*, www.theguardian.com, 29 May 2011.

1  Following Henry C. K. Liu, I consider the term 'sovereign debt' in relation to the Eurozone crisis grossly misleading since Eurozone member countries do not have any 'sovereign' control over the common currency, which is in reality controlled by the ECB. This means that 'sovereign debt' for each member state is denominated in what is, essentially, a foreign currency.

2  Capital imports are usually identical in size to current account deficits.

3  Yanis Varoufakis, *And the Weak Suffer What They Must: Europe, Austerity and the Threat to Global Stability* (London, 2016), p. 150.

4  'New money is principally created by commercial banks when they extend or create credit, either through making loans, including overdrafts, or buying existing assets. In creating credit, banks simultaneously create brand new deposits in our bank accounts, which, to all intents and purposes, is money.' Josh Ryan-Collins, Tony Greenham, Richard Werner and Andrew Jackson, *Where Does*

*Money Come From? A Guide to the* UK *Monetary and Banking System* (London, 2012), p. 6.

5   Hans Werner Sinn locates here one of the reasons for the eventual sovereign and private debt crisis that struck the Eurozone after 2010. He notes, for example, that 'the bubbles in Greece and Portugal would have hardly been possible [if] markets would have demanded risk premium early on, spoiling the debtor states' appetite for ever more foreign credit.' Hans-Werner Sinn, *The Euro Trap* (Oxford, 2014), p. 76. Interestingly, he seems to miss the fact that the elimination of such risk premium and the convergence of interest rates was the primary vehicle through which many countries were lured into joining the Eurozone, in exchange for providing a lucrative import market for export countries. The logic of the argument is similar to claiming that if the Eurozone had not been created, the Eurozone crisis would have been avoided too.

6   Mortgage interest rates, which were quite high before the introduction of the euro, were reduced by almost 6 per cent between 1995 and 2001.

7   This is not to say that housing prices in Greece did not experience an upswing trend at the time. From 1997 to 2007 housing prices went up almost 150 per cent; we should keep in mind, however, that for various historical reasons, home ownership in Greece was already close to 70 per cent even before the euro. The credit expansion that followed after the monetary union only increased this by roughly 10–15 per cent.

8   If someone is genuinely interested in knowing who has been 'living above their means' in Greece, they should check the balance sheets of all media conglomerates.

9   European Commission, Economic and Financial Affairs, *Economic Databases and Indicators*, AMECO, General Government Data, Spring 2016. In 2002 Greek gross debt was 104.9 per cent of GDP. In 2008 it had reached 109.4 per cent of GDP. In real value, the difference was close to €100 million, but we have seen how numbers become relevant only when it is politically convenient.

10  'The Sick Man of the Euro', *The Economist*, www.economist.com, 3 June 1999.

11  As a possible remedy for this, the *Economist* article essentially spelled out what was to become the Agenda 2010 programme that Chancellor Schröder would introduce some years later.

12  In order to make sure that the targets set by Maastricht would be the guidelines of economic policy from then on, a summit in 1996 brought about the Stability and Growth Pact, a supplement to Maastricht, in which member countries were obliged to have medium-term goals and budgetary measures that ensured their

compliance. If a member country failed to keep these promises, sanctions were supposed to follow. Interestingly, it was France and Germany who, responding to very low growth, combined forces to stop the imposition of sanctions in 2003.

13 China's impressive growth rates at the time meant an augmentation of its imports, something that contributed to the German export boom.

14 This official statement came from Jean Claude Trichet, president of the ECB, April 2007. Quoted in David Marsh, *The Euro: The Battle for the New Global Currency* (London, 2011), p. 241.

15 Ibid.

16 ECB, *Tenth Anniversary Monthly Bulletin* (2008), p. 83.

17 All this occurred in the aftermath of the anti-globalization movement, which had accused capitalist expansion of accelerating inequality and poverty on a global scale. Pointing at the global dynamism of the economy, institutions such as the IMF were claiming that, in fact, globalization was effectively moving in the opposite direction. As 60 per cent of world economic growth came from developing countries, this was reducing inequality faster than any of the protests.

18 In the past, the process of issuing housing loans was quite strict and strictly regulated. Only specific banks were allowed to offer such loans, and they rarely exceeded 60–70 per cent of the market price, the rest being the responsibility of the buyer. Moreover, banks were forced to keep sufficient reserves in their balance sheets to protect themselves from defaults. Starting from the late 1970s, the U.S. gradually abolished such 'hindrances' to capitalist expansion.

19 In 2007 sub-prime mortgage loans represented only 14 per cent of outstanding mortgages. Of these, only 3 per cent defaulted.

20 RMBS were packaged financial deals (such as loans) that banks sold to larger insurance companies. This allowed banks to void responsibilities from collecting payments on the loans.

21 This process increased public debt and deficits as governments added 'bail-out' funds to their balance sheets.

22 The immediate result was that investors abandoned the collapsed real-estate market and shifted their attention to the stock market, where shares had become quite attractive. Within a few months, they shifted again to the commodity markets. The increased speculation in that sector spiked prices, which, in turn, caused a global recession as demand plummeted. That was felt heavily in the developing world, sparking a series of protests that contributed greatly to the Arab Spring in 2011.

23 According to Sinn's pro-market ideological understanding, this was a case of 'undermining the fundamental role of the capital markets in assessing the risks and charging well-differentiated risk premia'.

Sinn, *The Euro Trap*, p. 77. Once again, Sinn offers a good example of what 'market fundamentalism' looks like.

24 The ECB would eventually be forced to start its own quantitative easing programme in 2015, which did, however, exclude countries, like Greece, who were most in need.

## 5 The 'Greek' Crisis

1 Part of this process meant that the ECB bought €33 billion worth of Greek bonds at 70 per cent of their value, bonds that would not have been sold for more than 10 per cent of their value in the market. This initial 'helping hand' towards Greece, called the Securities Market Programme (SMP), would later prove catastrophic: as the ECB mandate forbids losses, the Greek bonds held by the ECB would not be part of the haircut in 2012. As a result, Greece was forced to continue making interest payments for these exact bonds. In a recent letter, the President of the ECB, Mario Draghi, admitted that the ECB had received a €7.8 billion net interest income from these bonds (Letter QZ-064 from Mario Draghi to Nikolaos Chountis, 10 October 2017, www.ecb.europa.eu). Yanis Varoufakis claims in *Adults in the Room: My Battle with Europe's Deep Establishment* (London, 2017) that one of Greece's leverages against enforced capital controls by the ECB in 2015 was to default on these bonds.

2 The extent of exposure to the toxic RMBS was not yet entirely transparent. For this reason, banks used the money handouts to secure their positions and keep afloat, refraining from continuing their credit supply. This free money also meant that they were not pressured, as some argue that they should have been, to recapitalize (that is, forcing shareholders to dig deep in their pockets in order to balance their sheets).

3 Announced by the ECB in May 2010, the SMP (Securities Markets Programme) was a pro-active meant to ensure liquidity in 'malfunctioning segments of the debt securities markets'. It was ended in 2014.

4 In early October 2009 the Greek Statistical Authority had sent its biannual EDP (Excessive Deficit Procedure) report to Eurostat claiming a deficit of approximately 7 per cent. As this was almost double the April 2009 report, Eurostat asked for clarifications. The then-head of the Statistical Authority acknowledged some outstanding problems and requested an extension until the end of the year to revise the findings. Nonetheless, and literally only a few days after Papandreou's government won the elections, the new head of the Greek Statistical Authority issued a 'corrected' report, something that took Eurostat officials by surprise.

5 The debt ratio corresponds to my own calculations based on the official EDP reports of the Eurostat of 21 October 2009. A later report by ELSTAT (the renamed Statistical Authority) in October 2010 revalued the 2009 deficit at 15.4 per cent, putting the debt/GDP ratio at 127 per cent. By that time, Papandreou had appointed Andreas Georgiou as head of ELSTAT, a position he held simultaneously while serving as deputy chief of statistics for the IMF.

6 Merkel had already requested €406 billion to protect German markets from exposure to the U.S. derivatives market. For a brief but thorough analysis of the situation, see Mark Blyth, *Austerity: The History of a Dangerous Idea* (Oxford, 2013), esp. Chapter Three, 'Europe – Too Big to Bail: The Politics of Permanent Austerity', pp. 51–96.

7 European Commission, 'Report on Greek Government Deficit and Debt Statistics', Brussels, 8 January 2010, pp. 20–27.

8 The 'spread' of a bond represents the difference in interest between two set bonds. In the case of the Eurozone, the comparison is always between country x and German state bonds, as they are the most stable.

9 The story appeared in Kerin Hope, 'Greek Central Bank Faces Short Selling Claims', *Financial Times*, www.ft.com, 19 May 2010. Somewhat surprisingly, the article does not dwell at all on the tremendous implications that such a 'window' opens up for the veritable financial ruin of a national economy.

10 Even the European Commission Report is forced to note this, arguing that 'it is surprising that in spite of the information provided previously by the GAO [General Accounting Office] in October about the impossibility to conclude the work before the end of the year, it was seemingly possible to undertake it in only a few days after the change of government'; European Commission, 'Report on Greek Government Deficit and Debt Statistics', Brussels, 8 January 2010, p. 21.

11 According to this approach, Papandreou and his administration were eager to implement a specific restructuring of the Greek economy but were well aware that they lacked the political support (from both the Greek people and their own party mechanism) to enforce it. By handing out control of economic policy to external institutions, the implementation of this restructuring could proceed as an external obligation, potentially rendering their own political careers less exposed to criticism. Papandreou's belief in the necessity of the restructuring is not questionable: the deliberate choice to mess around with Greek statistics to achieve that might well be. In any case, Papandreou got his expressed wish, but the austerity that was imposed in Greece took its toll on him too. A year

and a half later, he would be forced to resign and would practically bid farewell to his political career.

12   The admission that statistical reports in Greece were doctored had two interesting side effects: on the one hand, it lent credence to the illusion that Greece was the only country that was messing around with its statistical numbers, a ridiculous claim. At the same time, this lack of transparency and potential corruption also contributed to the delegitimization of the whole political class and would reach explosive levels in 2011.

13   Theodoros Pagalos, a prominent member of PASOK, summarized this attitude in his infamous phrase 'we all ate [enjoyed] it *together*' ('μαζί τα φάγαμε'), a levelling statement that left perpetrators and victims, guilty and innocent, poor and rich sharing equal responsibility.

14   As we were later to discover, this was a mere show. Discussions around a Greek economic collapse and a subsequent request for foreign assistance between Papandreou and European/IMF officials were initiated months before Papandreou had won the elections. The former managing director of the IMF, Dominique Strauss-Kahn, admitted as much in an interview he gave to the French TV channel Canal+ in 2010.

15   Dr Schäuble has repeated this position ever since, to the detriment of successive Greek governments, as well as the Bundesbank, which has repeatedly explained that not only would the consequences of such a 'Grexit' be entirely unpredictable, but that Germany (especially back in 2010) would immediately record tremendous losses, as a Greek default would wipe out massive obligations to German banks. The insistence, at all times, that a potential Grexit could be well handled by the rest of the Eurozone seemed to ignore such calculations of the costs. Nonetheless, after 2012, when German and French exposure was eradicated, Schäuble could claim that he was vindicated.

16   Quantitative Easing refers to the process of a central bank directly purchasing assets from either the public or the private sector. It is meant to increase the money supply (liquidity), lower interest rates and promote lending by restoring confidence. It is also a process testifying to the role of the Central Bank as the lender of last resort, responsible for keeping the economy in a stable state.

17   Quoted in David Marsh, *The Euro: The Battle for the New Global Currency* (London, 2011), p. 249. According to Marsh, Merkel eventually vetoed the idea.

18   Even Germany recorded a 3.2 per cent deficit, despite efforts to maintain its 0.2 per cent surplus from 2007. At the same time, according to figures from Eurostat, Ireland had reached 13.8 per cent, Spain 11 per cent, Portugal 9.8 and France 7.2 per cent.

19  If, for example, a country reported a deficit of 6 per cent, nothing could stop it from issuing bonds worth 6 per cent of GDP to cover it. A survey of Eurozone members' deficit ratios in the 2000s, cross-referenced against yearly changes in the general government debt, reveals an uncanny correlation, a 'self-funding' operation that low interest rates made much easier.

20  Among other things, it had emerged that Greece's public debt was primarily short term, which meant that the government had costly upcoming obligations in the next few quarters. This partly explains the urgency of the situation. It also sheds light on the non-urgency in the case of Italy, which had, at the time, a debt/GDP ratio far larger than Greece's but which was of long-term maturity.

21  One should not ignore another crucial fact. Since the 1997 Asian crisis and Argentina's default in 2001, the IMF had seen its role and involvement seriously undermined as a result of the outright discrediting of its 'structural adjustment' programmes. A quick look at 'Past IMF Disbursements and Repayments for All Members from May 01, 1984 to April 30, 2017' (www.imf.org) reveals the obvious declining role of this historical institution until 2010.

22  It is quite puzzling and a sign of the confused times in which we are living that one has to clarify this. The Greek (Portuguese, Spanish, Irish and so on) economies were never given 'free handouts' at the expense of 'parsimonious taxpayers'. The capital transferred was in the form of loans with significant interest gains for creditors. Moreover, these loans have been used to service previous debt obligations, frequently to the same creditors, or to bail out insolvent banks that were, surely, quite high up in the list of those responsible for the economic breakdown. On the other hand, the populations that suffered through austerity and were not responsible for the previous financial collapse saw their wages, pensions and welfare repeatedly and systematically reduced, in order to pay past, present and future loans.

23  In what seems to have been a plan originating in France, the drawing up of bilateral loans meant that the burden for rescuing French and German banks fell 'equally' on all EMU member states.

24  In the end, only €73 billion belonging to this programme were disbursed, with the remaining €34.3 added to the second bail-out of 2012.

25  As Varoufakis rightly argues in *Adults in the Room*, repaying the loans was never, in fact, a priority for European officials.

26  The EFSF is yet another example of the hypocritical stance of the German monetary authorities. While publicly complaining about the burden of forthcoming bail-outs to national budgets, the EFSF was to be directly financed by European countries (and only partly by the IMF).

27 Jean Claude Trichet, as quoted by Tony Barber, *Financial Times*, 11 October 2010.

28 A few days after the signing, the following criticism appeared in an interview in *Der Spiegel*: '[The programme] was about protecting German banks, but especially the French banks, from debt write offs. On the day that the rescue package was agreed on, shares of French banks rose by up to 24 per cent. Looking at that, you can see what this was really about – namely, rescuing the banks and the rich Greeks.' Interestingly, this was not some lefty fanatic but former President of the Bundesbank Karl Otto Pöhl; see 'Bailout Plan is All about Rescuing Banks and Rich Greeks', *Der Spiegel*, www.spiegel.de, 18 May 2010.

## 6 Years of Stone

1 'Participation' in this case should be understood rather loosely, as it refers primarily to the number of people who took to the streets, not those who actively went on strike. One reason is that a systematic record of strike participation by the General Confederation of Unions only started in 2011. Second, even relying on official statistics for strike participation can be misleading: many people, especially from the private sector, would participate in demonstrations or strikes by calling in sick. Moreover, self-employed workers could abstain from working without their absence being recorded as an official strike.

2 A small historical note on the question of violence in Greek street protests is crucial. There exists in Greece considerable social tolerance of street violence during demonstrations and strikes, a legacy that comes straight from the experiences of the dictatorship. The strong shared dislike that most Greeks have for the police renders attacks against them somewhat justified. For its part, the riot police are notorious for indiscriminate violence against almost anyone who gets in their way, while their overgenerous use of tear gas in the centre of Athens effectively means that everyone gets a whiff of the repressive side of the state. In the previous two decades, violence against the riot police had effectively been monopolized by the radical/anarchist milieu, with direct participation in the violent confrontations by non-anarchists only occurring during a few moments of generalized social explosions. The struggles against austerity after 2010, themselves expressions of a massive social explosion, re-legitimized violent confrontations.

3 The European Commission's report briefly touched on these, making sure to overemphasize the thorny issue of 'wage increases' and 'loose fiscal policy'. In its introduction, we read, 'The strong growth perform-ance of Greece over the last decade was based on unsustainable

drivers . . . High real wage increases, rapid credit growth – supported by financial sector liberalization and low real interest rates associated with euro adoption – and loose fiscal policy contributed to buoyant growth.' European Commission, *The Economic Adjustment Program of Greece*, Occasional Papers 61 (May 2010), p. 3.

4 George Papaconstantinou, *Game Over: The Inside Story of the Greek Crisis* (CreateSpace, 2016), p. 64.

5 The actual increase in state spending for wages, pensions and 'other social programmes' (such as health) for 2000–2010 was €8.3 billion, or 3.6 per cent of GDP, and therefore below EU average (Eurostat; OECD). While complaining about this 3.6 per cent, Papaconstantinou saw no contradiction in 2010 in proposing a write-off of private companies' debts towards the state worth €24 billion (10.6 per cent of GDP).

6 Providing details might have forced them to acknowledge that one of the most significant sources of revenue loss for the Greek state has been the drastic reduction in corporate tax. Looking at the years between 2000 and 2010, for example, income from corporate taxation declined by almost 50 per cent (€5.1 billion in 2000, €3.1 billion in 2010), while taxation on individuals increased by almost 50 per cent (€5.4 billion in 2000, €9.4 billion in 2010). This interesting transformation took place while GDP went from €136 billion (2001) to €299.3 billion (2010), making it a period officially recorded as 'growth' and unofficially as increased capital profitability (data from Greek Ministry of Finance, https://tradingeconomics.com).

7 All countries that experienced the credit bubble discussed in Chapter Five had an inflation growth rate slightly larger than the average euro-area rate and marginally higher than the anti-inflation hysteria of Germany and the ECB, whose definition of acceptable inflation rates is 2 per cent. More significantly, perhaps, the whole euro-area recorded a notable increase in inflation immediately after the outbreak of the global crisis of 2007 and 2008, as all governments increased their deficit spending to counteract the effects of the downturn. For what it is worth, Greece has officially been in deflationary mode since 2013 (Eurostat, HICP Annual Rate of Change).

8 The sudden rise of Greek bond yields (as well as Spanish, Portuguese, Italian and so on) was already recorded immediately after the financial crisis of 2007–8 and explained by the so-called liquidity problem and the freezing of the interbank market in Europe. As the State Budget Report of the Greek Government for 2009 stated, '[the widening of the yields] was observed in all countries of the Eurozone, even those who had a higher rating of creditworthiness than Greece, and was not the result of a lack of confidence on behalf of investors, but in the closing of positions

and the mass liquidation of portfolio bonds from European and international institutional investors, with the aim of increasing liquidity' (State Budget 2009, p. 138). The Bank of Greece had a similar approach: 'The supply of government (and corporate) securities on the global market will increase significantly, as a result of the fiscal stimulus and bank liquidity support packages implemented in other countries; this will exert upward pressure on bond yields and possibly on yield spreads across individual countries and, as a result, raise the Greek government's borrowing costs' ('Summary of the Annual Report', Bank of Greece, 2009, p. 13).

9   Memorandum of Agreement, May 2010, p. 1.

10  In September 2010 French banks' exposure to the public sectors of Greece, Ireland, Portugal and Spain was $103.0 billion, while that of German banks amounted to $66.4 billion (Bank of International Settlements, BIS *Quarterly Review*, September 2010).

11  The Technical Appendix of the Agreement repeatedly asserts that (my emphasis): 'The primary expenditure of the central government that is monitored *excludes payments related to bank support*' (p. 19); 'The primary expenditure of the central government that is monitored for the Performance Criteria *excludes any cash payments related to bank restructuring*' (p. 20); 'For the purposes of the program, the ceiling on the stock of central government debt *will exclude debt arising from payments for bank restructuring*' (p. 21).

12  Memorandum of Agreement, May 2010, p. 2. The Memorandum Agreement announced the creation of a Greek Financial Stability Fund (FSF), responsible for providing 'liquidity' to the banks, with an immediate injection of €10 billion (from the €110 billion of the Troika). Adding the €28 billion they had already received (€10.5 billion in 2009 and another €17.5 billion in 2010), by July 2010 Greek banks had received €38 billion, approximately 16 per cent of GDP. At the same time, the ECB was accepting as collateral toxic bonds that were impossible to resell, but only insofar as the Greek state guaranteed them. This is the process through which private debt became public.

13  Since 2008 all Greek banks (with the sole exception of TT Hellenic Postbank) had an average of 110 per cent loan/asset ratio. To speak of liquidity problems was a remarkable euphemism.

14  Sotiropoulos, Milios and Lapatsioras have spotted an interesting contradiction arising in this discussion of 'competitiveness': 'When economic borders are open and capitalist firms are exposed to international competition, a general loss of competitiveness would be expressed in a reduced corporate profitability, declining productivity, lower growth rates, and higher unemployment growth in relation to inflation. [Yet] neither of these symptoms can be

observed for the countries of the European "periphery"'; Dimitris
P. Sotiropoulos, John Milios and Spyros Lapatsioras, *A Political
Economy of Contemporary Capitalism and its Crisis: Demystifying
Finance* (London, 2013), p. 193.

15  Anyone who has ever dealt with the public sector in Greece has
regretted the interaction. The relentless and irrational bureaucracy,
combined with the often visible indifference of the personnel,
makes targeting this sector quite easy. The historical and material
reasons behind this are, however, conveniently ignored. The
creation of the Greek state in the context of widespread local,
patriarchal and pre-capitalist relations was organized by the
establishment of a bureaucracy as a means to avoid the development of clientelism, which was seen as the natural by-product of
such social relations. The rushed introduction of such a bureaucratic apparatus on the model of Western European countries,
however, had the opposite result. It effectively gridlocked any
transaction with the public sector through unsurpassable bureaucratic barriers. The only way in which anything could be done was
precisely by circumventing the existing bureaucracy and resorting
to clientelist relations. Public sector workers in Greece are thus
consistently caught between two worlds: following impossible
bureaucratic rules or ignoring them by maintaining clientelist
relations.

16  It is absolutely imperative to add, however, that the majority of
those who proclaim their indignation towards the public sector
(politicians, journalists, academics) owe their existence, social
position and wealth to the public sector.

17  From 2009 a concerted campaign of discrediting the public sector
had been accelerated in the mainstream press, focusing on the
urban myth that the state did not even know how many people
it employed. See, for example, 'Κρύβουν τον αριθμό των δημοσίων
υπαλλήλων' ('They Are Hiding the True Number of Public
Employees'), *To Vima*, www.tovima.gr, May 2009 [Greek].

18  George Papandreou, Speech at the Digital Economy Forum,
3 May 2010 (my translation).

19  The number of public sector employees in Greece is available
in all portals of international institutions such as Eurostat, the
IMF, the World Bank and the OECD. Even if the Greek government
wanted to feign ignorance of these outlets, it could have easily
consulted the quarterly reports of its own Ministry of Interior.

20  A variety of estimates were offered to the eager public, but the
most impressive was that of 1,100,000 public workers. With a
population of 11 million, this number implied that a tenth of all
Greeks was in some form of wage dependency from the state
mechanism. Contrary to other imaginary numbers, this one carried

a 'scientific' stamp of approval, as it was published in a report by the Commercial and Industrial Chamber of Athens. When a team of investigative journalists asked to see the 'scientific' report, they were sent a one-page document with three paragraphs. The first paragraph merely stated the 'difficulty of knowing the exact number'. The second paragraph revealed its source to be 'a rough estimate', while the third paragraph based its findings on Wikipedia. See 'The Myth of Excessive Public Employees', *Ios*, www.iospress.gr, 19 September 2010 [Greek].

21 The size of the Greek public sector (in relation to percentage of workers employed, burden on government expenditure and so on) was, in fact, contrary to all propaganda, below the euro-area average. See Heinz Handler, Bertrand Koebel, Philipp Reiss and Margit Schratzenstaller, 'The Size and Performance of Public Sector Activities in Europe', WIFO Working Paper no. 246, February 2005.

22 The self-employed category in Greece is rather peculiar, as it bundles together a cross-class mix. It includes, among others, lawyers and doctors who run private offices and receive generous wages and unofficial bribes, successful architects, engineers and accountants, as well as their impoverished colleagues. It also contains a vast number of workers in diverse jobs, from waitresses and hairdressers to media workers, who are forced to register themselves as self-employed, thus allowing bosses to avoid paying for their social insurance. This wild bunch is mistakenly thought of as a coherent social category under the umbrella of 'self-employed'. From the point of view of the state, and the supposed crusade against tax evasion, the self-employed proved a useful enemy: exploiting the fact that some of them were actually in a position to understate their earnings dramatically (either because their bargaining power had allowed special deals with the state mechanism or simply because the nature of their work permitted them to do so), the attack on this sector has been phenomenal. What also worked in favour of the austerity proponents was the fact that the 'self-employed' share no common ground but are rather broken down into many different and often antagonistic categories.

23 Most commentators (and critics) of Syntagma seem to forget that just two weeks before, neo-Nazis and like-minded patriots had orchestrated a veritable racist pogrom in the centre of Athens, by exploiting the brutal murder of a man by two people whose ethnic origin somehow became explanatory for the crime. Though neo-Nazis (like Golden Dawn) were clearly instigating these mobilizations, it was disturbing to see how many non-Nazis were willing to find some 'justification' for these events. This was the first appearance of the idiotic argument that migrants were somehow responsible

for the crisis. Nonetheless, as soon as the Syntagma Square occupation started, this mobilization was forgotten and ignored. For this reason, organized neo-Nazis publicly declared their opposition to the Syntagma occupation and urged their members to stay away from those 'corrupt' and 'anti-patriotic' demonstrators. Contrary to what most left-wing commentators have been saying ever since, the neo-Nazis of Golden Dawn were very much aware that a mobilization with the characteristics of Syntagma was entirely against their interests.

24  Initially, most anarchist/radicals refrained from participating in the Syntagma movement. Unfortunately, even when some of them decided to get their hands dirty and join the protests, most of them did so by entertaining a secret desire to 'teach' proper radical politics to the ignorant masses.

25  For example, many have made a big deal about the presence of Greek flags during the protests. I consider this a non-issue, not because the portrayal of a national symbol is irrelevant to the content of a struggle, but merely because the number of flags in relation to the amount of people present was totally insignificant. National politics were present in the square, of course, but one does not need to point at flags to show that. A closer look at the vision and perspective of the Left and their proud declarations of patriotism (of an anti-imperialist flavour, of course) is enough. Apart from the accepted category of the 'patriot', the reality on the square was that whenever nationalists, fascists or neo-Nazis were spotted, they were attacked, beaten up and eventually saved by the police. The notion that there was a widespread tolerance of nationalists and fascists is a myth, mostly repeated by people who never set foot on Syntagma Square.

26  On a similar note, one finds constant complaints about the 'passivity' of the masses. It is probably self-evident that the recent far-right mobilizations around the world should make these commentators wish for a return to 'passivity'.

27  It is along these lines that Varoufakis has structured his post-finance ministry activities. His 'movement' (in reality, a collection of celebrity intellectuals and their followers) has as its direct aim the 'democratization' of the Eurogroup, as if he considers it impossible for austerity to be democratically mandated. Though knowledgeable in economics, Varoufakis's attempts to win a spot in the political arena show a profound ignorance of how actual movements work.

28  Quite surprisingly, elements of the radical/anarchist factions also felt threatened by this, though it remains an undeniable part of their history to denounce and fight against the very same political organizations or institutions.

29  The failure of the Left in contemporary times should also be explained by the dominance (and fetishism) of the Gramscian

notion of 'hegemony'. Obsessed with the desire to produce intellectuals who will create a new 'hegemonic' discourse, they have lost track of the social antagonisms that capital produces. When the Right fills in this gap (for example with a Trump), they are forced to rediscover the material basis of class conflict that their ideological endeavours urged them to forget.

30 For example, Syriza's traditional fetishism of non-violence, a result of their parliamentary aspirations and a historically embedded ideology, felt entirely out of place (sometimes even to Syriza members themselves) when the overwhelming majority in the square was preoccupied with defending its existence from violent police attacks.

31 A specific example might clarify this: in the first few days of the Syntagma occupation, a veritable army of food carts parked on the square and proceeded to do great business with the thousands of hungry protesters. At a certain point the stench of the cooking, as well as the fact that they occupied too much space, led to a proposal in the open assembly to kick them out. Arguments in favour or against were discussed and the issue was brought to a vote. An overwhelming majority of hands were raised to expel the food carts from the square, but the aspiring bureaucrat who had taken control of the microphone did her best to cancel the vote and sabotage the decision. The assembly voted on the matter four times: on each occasion it became clear that people did not want those wagons, but the bureaucrat always came up with a new technicality that, in her view, rendered the vote invalid. Given that this was still the beginning, and the people were not yet weary of such mind-numbing idiocies, which were precisely intended to exhaust people into capitulation, she eventually had to back down. Two days later it became known that the food-wagon entrepreneurs had made a deal with the organizing committee to provide their members with free food during the protest.

32 Three out of the four speakers (Varoufakis, Katrougalos, Tsakalotos) ended up as ministers in the Syriza government of 2015.

33 This ridiculous idea was, of course, revived by the Syriza government, under the guise of a legally sound (and therefore safe) and moral demand. The only glitch is that it is nonsense. International law allows for the declaration of certain loans as odious, but only when they have been made by a recognized dictatorship or drawn up 'against the interests of the people'. The relentless ambiguity of such a claim is perfectly fitted to the Left's legalist fetish but remains extraneous to a social movement fighting against austerity.

34 The Invisible Committee, *To Our Friends* (Cambridge, MA, 2015), p. 31.

35 According to police reports, on 28 June 2011 alone they used 2,860 tear gas canisters, nearly emptying their reserves. On the same night, new orders for 10,000 canisters was placed in Israel, Germany

and France at a cost of €900,000. Word on the streets was that the new measures were voted in by the riot cops, not the MPS.

36 There is no 'democratic legitimacy' in attempting to blockade a parliament in order to obstruct the passage of legislation, nor can one find democratic credentials in violent acts of self-defence against the police forces. But as a teacher had remarked in 1998, 'There is no democracy. There is only strike.'

37 It is not only PASOK and New Democracy that have been inextricably tied with austerity but the smaller parties that lent a helping hand when necessary. LAOS was a populist, far-right offshoot from New Democracy, whose leader (K. Karatzaferis) was mostly interested, in a very indiscreet way, in securing some position of power within any government. The Democratic Left (DIMAR), on the other hand, was an offshoot of 'moderates' from Syriza. The role of both of these insignificant parties was to ensure the continuation of austerity by providing support to the government. As soon as this role was no longer necessary, they both receded into insignificance. Other political parties with similar aspirations have emerged, such as Potami, but their expediency is directly related to their usefulness.

38 Kotouza, 'Surplus Citizens', p. 156.

39 This specific struggle is of particular importance as it is a concentrated example of the earlier suggestion that austerity was fought at many different levels at the same time (and from different perspectives). In September 2011 then Finance Minister Evangelos Venizelos announced a new property tax (ENFIA), which would be collected through the electricity bill, accompanied by the threat that failure to pay the tax would result in the electricity being cut off. Resistance to the veritable poll tax was manifold: at an uncoordinated individual level (due to the inability or the refusal to pay); at a collective level (through neighbourhood assemblies); at a syndicalist level (the trade union of the Public Electricity Company initially tried to block the issuing of bills, only later to change its focus and denounce 'corruption'); at the level of political parties (Syriza and KKE declared their opposition to the law and claimed to support those who did not pay it, as did New Democracy before it was elected into government in June 2012); and at an institutional level (the law was brought to the highest court of Greece, which declared its existence legal but its collection through the electricity bill unconstitutional). Nonetheless, the fear attached to having your electricity cut off worked and the majority paid their bills, providing the government with €2.6 billion income in the first year. As such, the Troika rejected any suggestion of scrapping the law, forcing New Democracy quickly to abandon its pre-election promise. After 'negotiations' between New Democracy and the Troika, the 'compromise' reached was to keep the law but change its name.

40  Essentially the law brought together property owners, liable for its payment. This category may be rather misleading for foreign audiences who are not aware that 85 per cent of the population of Greece owns their house or apartment. It does, however, put some limitations on the scope and content of the movement.

41  An alternative currency does not challenge the existence of money but actually seeks to reinforce it by making some other currency available when the official, state-guaranteed one is in short supply. As such, it merely seeks to increase economic activity within a clearly defined community, without, however, cutting off relations with capitalist activity prior or external to this community. In the case of alternative exchange structures (often through providing labour in exchange for specific goods) which promise 'fair' exchanges, a certain equivalence inherited from the 'outside' world is presupposed, thus reinforcing the socially necessary average, which is the fundamental basis of capitalist exchange. In both of these cases, property relations (that is, class relations) remain identical. A similar point goes for time banks. Here, the value of abstract labour is directly related to its temporal (concrete) expression following a process that, due to its informality, remains random. As Kotouza rightly observes in her interesting critique and analysis, it is quite bizarre that the above activities were considered acts of 'solidarity', a notion that describes a mutuality between people with common interests, who expect nothing in return and refuse to qualify their acts on the basis of an abstract equivalence; see Kotouza, 'Surplus Citizens', pp. 159–67.

42  The choice, for example, on whether to budget medical supplies on the basis of the year they were received or on the year they were paid is a typical trick utilized by governments who wish to hide or reveal deficit spending. Needless to say, this form of creative accounting is not a Greek speciality.

43  According to an OECD paper, Greece had 'the highest rates in the EU on MRI units (22.6 per million population) and CT scanners (34.3 per million population), on MRI and CT exams (97.9 and 320.4 per 1000 population, respectively), and on the antibiotics' consumption (dose of 39 per 1000 population per day).' Effie Simou and Eleni Koutso-georgou, 'Effects of the Economic Crisis on Health and Healthcare in Greece in the Literature from 2009 to 2013: A Systematic Review', *Health Policy*, no. 115 (2014), pp. 111–19.

44  The data for this part comes from the extensive research commis-sioned by INE/GSEE: Sofia Adam and Dora-Dimitra Teloni, 'Social Health-clinics in Greece during the Crisis: The Experience of Providing Care as the National Health System Collapses', November 2015 [Greek].

45  A 24 per cent rise in admissions at public hospitals occurred at the same time as a 25 per cent decrease in the private sector.

46   It cannot be stressed enough how the deterioration of the health
     system has an even greater impact on women, as women's health
     is largely based on prevention through annual or semi-annual
     medical examinations. Moreover, and reflecting the already
     gendered division of labour, increasing unemployment affects
     women more, which means that more women found themselves
     without insurance.
47   See Adam and Teloni, 'Social Health-clinics in Greece', p. 113.
     As one participant argued, 'we are fighting for our self-abolition'.
     On another interesting note, however, many also responded that
     the experience had taught them that it is possible to de-commodify
     health care and introduce humane interactions between patients
     and health personnel, an experience they would like to inject back
     into public healthcare.
48   This level of participation urged some commentators to call the
     strike 'the mother of all strikes' of the period.
49   In the past, the KKE used to participate in the same demonstrations
     as everyone else, but its open hostility towards anyone outside its
     own bloc led to many conflicts that often turned violent, especially
     between KKE and anarchists. Due to its use of heavy-built
     construction workers and a certain discipline, the KKE used to come
     out on top in these fights, often handing over the anarchists to the
     police (while accusing them of being agent provocateurs). Towards
     the late 1990s, however, this strategy was becoming more fragile and
     the KKE decided to abandon joint demonstrations altogether and
     assemble its followers in separate locations.
50   Belgium was still licking the wounds of the collapse of the financial
     house Dexia, while Cyprus's financial troubles would start the same
     year but reach their critical point in 2013.
51   A breakdown of the Eurozone in such a way would immediately
     mean that the exposure of banks from core countries towards the
     periphery would cause a massive devaluation of currency (nothing
     less than 30 per cent according to most estimates). For France, to
     take the example of the country that suggested this very option, this
     meant the immediate need to cover €700 billion in losses (in 2011
     France's exposure was broken down to €415 billion to Italy, €150
     billion to Spain, €55 billion to Greece, €32 billion to Ireland, €25
     billion to Portugal and €23 billion to Belgium). Where would France
     get this money? It would have to borrow it. And who would lend it
     at a time when France's public debt was already at 85 per cent of
     GDP? Losses of €700 billion would automatically mean the increase
     of the public debt/GDP ratio to 110 per cent. It seems more plausible
     that Sarkozy came up with this idea out of fear that Germany might
     decide to go it alone, without France. But Germany would also not
     benefit from such an arrangement: though its banks were less

exposed, the losses they would incur due to exchange rate depreciation would hit their exports heavily, with some estimates putting it at about €250 billion.

52   The year 2011 closed with the Greek public debt at €375 billion, according to the finance ministry. By that time, the IMF had already started complaining that Greece's debt was becoming unsustainable, a predicament that, according to their mandate, forbade them from participating in any further bail-out programmes.

53   In the end, as with the first bail-out, €18.8 billion was not disbursed. Also in February 2015, the Hellenic Financial Stability Fund (HFSF) returned €10.9 billion to the EU. This brought the total disbursed amount to €153.8 billion.

54   Total debt at the moment was valued at €376 billion.

55   In the case of many of these funds, they were not even told that bonds they were holding were submitted to the haircut. In the following months it was revealed that some social insurance funds had lost so much money that they were unable to pay out pensions or provide healthcare to their clients.

56   For example, people like Evangelos Venizelos, former deputy prime minister and minister of finance (June 2011–March 2012), and short-term president of PASOK (2012–15). The importance of the PSI agreement for Venizelos and his career is such that he recently felt forced to publish a book attempting to defend its implementation. The title (and the dates covered) are indicative: Evangelos Venizelos, *Myths and Realities Concerning the Public Debt, 2012–2017* (Athens, 2017).

57   Most of Greece's public debt (First Memorandum, ECB, Treasury bills, and so on) was tied to interest rates with an average of 4.2 per cent. The PSI did, in fact, lower interest rate payment for the first three years after 2012, bringing them down to €11 billion a year. Since this amount corresponded to 5.5 per cent of GDP, the 'celebrated' restructuring is hardly relevant (in 2009, for example, interest payments were 5.1 per cent of GDP).

58   LTRO (towards banks) had a 1 per cent interest rate, as opposed to the EFSF (towards governments), which demanded 4 per cent.

59   Alternatively, foreclosure of the houses or apartments of those who did or could not repay their loans could potentially allow them to sell the properties at higher prices and thus make up the difference. For all these possibilities, economic recovery was presupposed – but it did not arrive.

60   This process was accelerated by the introduction of the LTRO mechanism discussed above.

61   These were also the main guidelines of Syriza's economic programme, as drafted by Yanis Varoufakis, which promised an end to austerity.

## 7 After the End

1   After the Troika was informed of the government's plans to replace the property tax law, they argued that if the government was in a position to find the €2.6 billion in income that the property tax had brought, they were willing to consider the option. Otherwise, they reminded Samaras, 'one does not change a winning horse'. New Democracy then tasked Finance Minister Stournaras with the responsibility of providing an alternative plan. When the Troika sent its task force to discuss the issue, Stournaras had nothing to show. They therefore agreed to continue with the same law and the same variables, but to change its name.

2   'Uncontrolled migration' is a choice of words that is, to say the least, insulting and grossly inadequate to describe the reality of what migrants and refugees experience in a journey characterized by constant border controls, police and military supervision, human traffickers, bureaucracy and humiliation at every step.

3   To mention just a small example, Antonis Samaras complained during a pre-election interview on national television that there were no longer any places for Greek children in the country's kindergartens, as these had been taken over by the children of immigrants. In the same interview, he called for the need to 'take back the cities that had been occupied by illegal immigrants'.

4   Comprised mostly of Afghans, Pakistanis and Iraqis, these migrants were stuck in Greece while desperately looking for a way to continue their journey towards central and northern Europe, with no intention whatsoever of staying in Greece. The result was that many of them ended up living in the streets or crammed in apartments in the poorer parts of Athens.

5   This can only be a surprise for those who have never seriously looked at questions of migration and 'integration'. Though Albanians were systematically and continuously exploited during the 1990s, significant numbers remained in Greece and had been integrated. This 'successful' integration or, in other words, the 'normalization' of their exploitation made some of them prone to over-identify with their new communities and to look down on newly arrived migrants.

6   Post-election analyses pointed out that support for Golden Dawn was predominantly concentrated in areas that traditionally vote for New Democracy. Another interesting fact is that Golden Dawn received close to 50 per cent of the votes in those areas where police security forces vote.

7   The interim government of Papademos had also had its fair share of racist rhetoric. Only a few months before, in April 2012, Minister of

Health Andreas Loverdos and Minister of Public Order Michalis Chrisochoidis, who were both members of PASOK, staged a joint press conference in which they unashamedly claimed that the collapse of the health system in Greece was the result of the free treatment of migrants. Moving on, they also argued that illegal migration had created a 'hygienic bomb' ready to explode in the urban centres. To support this racist delirium further, they announced that a number of illegal immigrant sex workers had been arrested, with the main charge against them being that they had knowingly attempted to infect their clients with HIV by insisting on unprotected sexual contact. Shortly after the press conference, the media were handed out pictures of these women, which they happily broadcast on national TV.

8   In reality, the effectiveness of the crackdown was as real as the threat it was meant to respond to: in other words, almost non-existent. Initially publishing frequent data on their operations, the police were eventually forced to cease these disclosures when it became obvious that the propaganda of an uncontrolled influx of illegal immigration did not match their results. For example, the last published official report showed that of the 90,000 people who had been stopped in the streets, only 5,000 were arrested. The only 'crime' of the over-whelming majority had been a lack of legal documents.

9   With a certain painful irony, Germany's approach to crisis management has been trapped since 2010 in a gridlock that is a result of its own propaganda. Forever insisting on the argument that Germany's taxpayers are being asked to give free hand-outs to lazy, uncompetitive Southern Europeans, any change in the programme, aims and direction of restructuring would be interpreted as giving in to the South. For Germany, thus, the only option that exists is the continuation of the existing agreed programmes, despite their miscalculations, mistakes and/or false projections. Any alternative to that would have to be renegotiated inside the German parliament, risking significant losses for the Christian Democratic Union ruling party. All of this is notwithstanding their ideological commitment to recessionary policies.

10  Apart from providing a short-fused lifeline to the crumbling government of Mario Monti, another decision of the EU Summit that was met with relief by everyone except Germany and its allies (Finland, Slovakia and the Netherlands) was the signing of the Compact for Growth and Jobs, whose aim was to reassure Eurozone governments that growth was still on the agenda by injecting €120 billion into the European economy. For further details on this EU Summit, see Janis A. Emmanouilidis, 'The Prospects of Ambitious Muddling Through: The Results of an EU Summit in Deep Crisis Mode', European Policy Centre, www.epc.eu, 2 July 2012.

11 According to Wolfgang Schäuble, the ECB's supervision 'should focus its direct oversight on those banks that can pose a systemic risk at a European level. This is not just in line with the tested principle of subsidiarity. It is also common sense; we cannot expect a European watchdog to supervise directly all of the region's lenders – 6,000 in the Eurozone alone – effectively.' Wolfgang Schäuble, 'How to Protect EU Taxpayers Against Bank Failures', *Financial Times*, www.ft.com, 30 August 2012. This same argument has been the main obstacle against the long-awaited 'Banking Union' within the Eurozone.

12 The ECB directly hinted at the danger of a collapse of the EMU, but it hid this threat behind technocratic jargon. Draghi thus spoke about the 'convertibility risk' of the Euro currency, which means nothing less than the fear of the Euro being converted to national currencies, i.e. the break-up of the EMU.

13 Quantitative Easing is a process through which a central bank buys bonds issued from the public and private sector. To avoid the accusation of direct financing of states and private companies, which is forbidden by the ECB's constitution, the ECB does not register itself as a direct buyer but only purchases from the secondary market. For many, this is purely a technocratic excuse, as primary buyers are well aware that bonds will be purchased directly from the ECB and therefore set their offers accordingly. In any case, immediately after Draghi's announcement, the interest of Spain's ten-year bonds dropped from 7.64 per cent to 5.62 per cent, while the equivalent Italian one fell from 6.6 per cent to 5.03 per cent.

14 European Commission, 'Executive Summary', The Second Economic Adjustment Programme for Greece: First Review, December 2012.

15 'An Amazing Mea Culpa from the IMDF's Chief Economist on Austerity', *Washington Post*, 3 January 2013. For the IMF's full text, see Olivier Blanchard and Daniel Leigh, *Growth Forecast Errors and Fiscal Multipliers*, NBER Working Paper 18779, National Bureau of Economic Research, www.nber.org, February 2013. In summary, the IMF had wrongly calculated that cuts in public spending equivalent to 1 per cent of GDP contribute to 0.5 per cent growth.

16 This choice was surely also inspired by the fact that the Cypriot banking sector, and its offshore tax haven, was a favourite destination of Russian business, both legal and otherwise. In any case, the singling out of Cyprus on the basis of an over-bloated financial sector received angry criticism from similar countries; Luxembourg's foreign minister, Jean Asselborn, for example, warned Berlin that it needed to 'watch its words, as no one was complaining that the German car or arms industries were too big'; Ian Traynor, 'Cyprus's Banks Have Been Tamed – Are Malta and Luxembourg Next?', *The Guardian*, www.theguardian.com, 25 March 2013.

17  The value of a currency gets adversely affected when its owner has no access to it as a result of capital controls, the decrease of the money supply or other reasons. When a Cypriot cannot access her savings, this is tantamount to saying that she does not have these savings. The situation prompted economist Karl Whelan to ask 'Has Cyprus already left the Euro?', *Forbes*, www.forbes.com, 28 March 2013.

18  While it is true that certain sectors of the self-employed had managed to have significant tax gifts due to their relations to the government, the accusation that the self-employed sector as a whole was characterized by such allowances was a smokescreen. In reality, the government was conforming to the Troika demand to reduce the self-employed sector and continue a process of transformation of self-employed to wage-labourers.

19  'Executive Summary', Second Review of the 2nd Economic Adjustment Programme, May 2013, p. 3.

20  Ibid., p. 4.

21  A 'low concentration of capital' is economic jargon for the existence of a large network of small companies with small capital. Greece was a particularly obvious example, with almost 95 per cent of businesses employing fewer than ten people.

22  The official excuse was that ERT was a castle of public sector corruption and a major burden on the state budget. In reality, ERT steadily recorded surpluses and had no connection whatsoever to the state budget. It was paid directly from people's electricity bills, and the cost for each household was €4.24 per month, or else €50.88 per year.

23  In this process, a more radical faction of those supporting the occupation of the building suggested that its employees should open the doors to everyone and start broadcasting a new programme, one that would highlight and connect existing struggles against austerity. But the doors were never opened. Using the excuse of fears about the expensive equipment inside, the union-led personnel trying to take charge of the situation rejected such proposals, preferring to have people sitting outside listening to music and speeches. Eventually, after it was obvious that the unions were only interested in passive spectators of 'their' struggle, the majority of supporters left the streets.

24  The preparation for government was surely an important factor in their decision. But one should not deduce their attitude merely from this. Syriza never had radical political pretensions and their attitude in the few trade unions in which they had some representation was more or less always the same.

25  One year before, a ten-month strike and workplace occupation organized by a KKE-led union in a key copper factory in Athens had also been evicted by riot police.

26 According to OECD data, general government spending rose from 55.42 per cent of GDP in 2012 to 62.29 per cent in 2013. Similarly, the Government deficit increased from 8.89 per cent of GDP to 13.15 per cent. This increase was even larger than the one recorded between 2004 and 2009, when general government spending had risen from 47.61 per cent to 54.08 per cent; OECD, Data, General Government Spending, Total, % of GDP, 2000–2015.

27 Initiated in 2012, the OMT (Outright Monetary Transactions) programme allowed the ECB to make sovereign bond purchases in the secondary markets. As noted, countries undergoing structural adjustment programmes were excluded.

28 Varoufakis makes a valid point in *Adults in the Room: My Battle with Europe's Deep Establishment* (London, 2017): Greece also recorded a primary surplus in its current account in 1943, during the Nazi occupation, when imports were crippled.

29 Since then this 'success story' has been the battle flag of New Democracy and most pro-austerity pundits. Ever since the election of Syriza, the so-called 'success story' of 2013 has been used as a rallying point, supposedly indicating that the Greek economy was on a path back to growth that was rudely interrupted by the Syriza and ANEL government. In reality, however, the argument is extremely flawed: instead of recognizing that the continued economic collapse of the Greek economy is a direct result of the continuation of the austerity programme, the proponents of this approach claim that the problem lies with Syriza and ANEL's inability actually to implement austerity. The government's performance since 2015 has shown that the exact opposite is true.

30 Kerin Hope, 'Greece Defies Troika with the New Budget', *Financial Times*, www.ft.com, 21 November 2014.

31 It is worth noting that many of Syriza's proposals stem directly from the Troika's own admissions of mistakes and miscalculations. What Varoufakis did as finance minister, at least in the beginning, was simply to make public what was, up to that point, only permitted to circulate in private: that the debt was not sustainable, that internal devaluation was only deepening the recession, that cutting wages, especially in the public sector, would necessarily collapse demand. This is another straightforward way for people to understand that there was nothing particularly 'radical' about Syriza's programme.

32 Ludwig Feuerbach, *The Essence of Christianity*, Preface to 2nd edn of 1843 (Leipzig, 2008).

33 An analytical report on the details and inconsistencies of the Thessaloniki programme can be found in my article: Pavlos Roufos, 'Is it Possible to Win the War after Losing All the Battles?', *Brooklyn Rail*, www.brooklynrail.org, 5 February 2015.

34  Already from October 2012, Georgios Stathakis, Syriza's top economist and growth strategist, had declared that the best strategy for overcoming the crisis had three pillars: freezing wages and public spending at existing levels, solving the problems of the banking sector and seeking fast-track investment opportunities; Georgios Stathakis, 'Changes Against the Memorandum', *To Vima* [The Tribune], www.tovima.gr, 21 October 2012 [Greek].

35  'When the debt is rendered viable again with a deal that a strong Syriza government can bring, the markets will start lending to Greece at a reasonable interest rate'; Georgios Stathakis, 'Negotiation of the Agreement – Cancellation of the Memorandum', *Naftemporiki*, www.naftemporiki.gr, 22 December 2014. These are the most material examples of how Syriza's vision was modelled on a return to the past, in this case, the glorious days of credit expansion as a model of economic 'growth' and accumulation.

36  Syriza shamelessly described the exposure of the bankruptcy of the banking sector as a *pretext* for its takeover by foreign interests. Leaving aside the calculated fallacy of suggesting that any foreign investor would be interested in investing in an insolvent banking sector, the key to explaining Syriza's assertion was by seeing it as an echo of the constant fear of Greek bank managers and CEOs: a failure to raise 10 per cent of its re-capitalization needs would mean that management would have to be handed over to the state.

37  As an example, even before it was elected to government, Syriza's prominent member Rena Dourou, who had been elected chief of the municipality of Attica, which includes Athens, gave a gift of €20 million to G. Melissanidis, a shipping magnate and oil tycoon.

38  Syriza's pre-election promises were optimistically calculated at €12 billion. To the extent that the Troika could freely interpret any action of the Greek government as non-compliant to the existing programme and close down its banks, there was little point in the programme itself.

39  The illusion of European agreement to an easing of the restructuring process was, one has to admit, maintained by the stance of a number of European officials who played along with Syriza's emphasis on growth instead of austerity, though none of them ever touched on the issue of debt restructuring. These voices of support came primarily from the European Commission, in statements by politicians such as Pierre Moscovici and Jean-Claude Juncker.

40  Though many of the suggestions had a Keynesian flavour, Varoufakis refrained from billing their cost to further state/deficit spending, opting instead for a middle ground of financing the New Deal from the interest paid by commercial banks to the European System of Central Banks and from Target II obligations. These proposals can be found in Varoufakis's blog, his online articles from 2010 to 2014

and in the evolving versions (from November 2010) of *A Modest Proposal for Resolving the Eurozone Crisis*, co-written initially with Stuart Holland and later also with James K. Galbraith, available at www.yanisvaroufakis.eu, accessed 22 February 2018.

41 This has been spelled out often in this book but perhaps a repetition here is timely: massively increasing an already high public debt in order to save the private, failing, banking sector, the excuse of 'sovereign debt' was used in order to exclude Eurozone member states from the market, imposing a set of harsh restructuring based on the essentials of the Maastricht Treaty, in exchange for keeping them from defaulting.

42 This was clearly a politically motivated decision. In 2012 Draghi had agreed to increase the number of Treasury bills that the ECB would accept as collateral to help Samaras's government.

43 Almost a month before Syriza won the election, the governor of the Bank of Greece (an ECB branch, for all purposes) had done something unbelievably detrimental to the economy and contrary to any formal understanding of the role of a national Central Bank: he had initiated a bank run. In a public statement on 15 December 2014 he argued, 'In the context of my duties as governor of the Bank of Greece, and in my capacity as a member of the Governing Board of the European Central Bank, I must note that the crisis of the last days is becoming serious, that liquidity in markets is diminishing at a high rate and that the risk, not only of the reduction in economic growth that recently restarted but also the irreversible impairment of the Greek economy, is large.' Yannis Stournaras, 'Xenophon Zolotas: Parallels and Lessons from Back then for Today', 15 December 2014, quoted in Varoufakis, 'Adults in the Room', p. 512.

44 Varoufakis has often contradicted himself, sometimes even about entirely irrelevant things. Focusing on this is, however, rather pointless because the arena of political 'debates' was nothing more than a spectacular show with little, if any, relevance to reality. If Varoufakis could be reproached with something more specific, it would probably be the fact that he acted as if he was finance minister of the Eurozone *as a whole* and not simply of Greece. His strategy of negotiation was entirely consistent with his writings of recent years, but giving lectures on the faulty architecture of the Eurozone to European bureaucrats and offering proposals that presupposed a change of course for the Monetary Union as a whole was essentially nonsensical. What Varoufakis failed to recognize was that the continuation of austerity was not a mathematical error, which could be corrected once the Troika recognized his superior proposals, but the essence of the programmes, irrespective of their actual effects on the Greek economy or any consideration of the sustainability of the debt.

45 The actual question of the referendum was whether Greek citizens agreed or not with a Troika draft proposal titled 'Reforms for the completion of the current programme', which was a 23-page document of economic jargon and incomplete numbers, as well as another draft paper titled 'Preliminary Debt Sustainability Analysis', which examined various scenarios in relation to the Greek public debt. The notion that 'Greek citizens' would be in a position to decipher the jargon of the first text was ridiculous. The proposal to vote 'Yes' or 'No' to a series of different scenarios was even more absurd.

46 This was not an obvious miscalculation. Despite seven years of catastrophic austerity, Greeks have remained overwhelmingly and consistently in favour of membership of the Eurozone. As *The Economist* has astutely described, countries at the receiving end of harsh restructuring tend to view Eurozone membership as a condition similar to Alcatraz, 'a prison that keeps people in mainly by making escape too risky'; 'Special Report: The Future of the European Union', *The Economist*, 25 March 2017.

47 This did not mean, however, that the government enjoyed the trust of the public. At the same time as big mobilizations for a 'No' vote were taking place, there was a massive deposit outflow, further draining banks.

48 The third bail-out, signed on July 2015, promised the disbursement of €86 billion in the course of the next three years. The loan was handled by the ESM (without the IMF providing any additional loans) and it was broken down to €35.9 billion for debt amortization, €17.8 billion for interest payment on existing debt, €7 billion for clearances and, of course, €25 billion for bank recapitalization.

49 'At the time of its inception, the Treuhand assumed ownership of approximately 95 per cent of the enterprise sector, comprising some 9,000 industrial firms, 20,000 commercial enterprises, 7,500 hotels and restaurants and 40 per cent of the total land area, with a total employment of 3 million'; Rudiger Dornbusch and Holger C. Wolf, 'East German Economic Reconstruction', in *The Transition in Eastern Europe*, ed. Olivier Jean Blanchard, Kenneth A. Froot and Jeffrey D. Sachs, vol. I (Chicago, IL, 1994), pp. 155–90. Within four years, more than 14,600 companies and parts of companies had been privatized, while 3,700 others were liquidated. In the process, 2.6 million workers lost their jobs.

50 The government of Syriza-ANEL has continued, until this very day, to promise that debt restructuring is around the corner.

51 Varoufakis was *post facto* credited not only with the failure of the 'negotiations', but with the harshness of the new set of measures. He was also accused of both not having a plan B in place and, once his plan B was revealed, for having one.

52 'Greece: Request for Extended Arrangement under the Extended Fund Facility', IMF Country Report No. 12/57, March 2012, p. 49.

53 Greece is not the focus of Sinn's book. It is rather to repeat the approach that the architecture of the Eurozone forces surplus countries to bear the burden of deficit countries, especially those that refused to exercise fiscal discipline. After critiquing the temporary (EFSF) and permanent (ESM) rescue mechanisms, Sinn also takes aim at what was at the time a developing policy of the ECB: quantitative easing. In typical market fundamentalist fashion, Sinn argues that this policy does not allow for the necessary 'clearing out' of the market from non-competitive companies or extremely risk-prone banks. Essentially, however, the ultimate target in his book is the Target II system, the interbanking system of the Eurozone. Using data that show Target II obligations towards Germany in a sudden hike since 2010, Sinn concludes that Target II has consistently been used as a backdoor bail-out mechanism, beyond the control and supervision of the EC, the ECB or other authorities. What Sinn suspiciously fails to notice, however, is that the increased obligations towards Germany represent the capital that German investors had sent to the periphery before the crisis, due to slightly higher yields, and which was now returning to Germany. These capital transfers were only possible precisely because the ECB, which Sinn criticizes, treated all such obligations/bonds as good as gold. Had the ECB followed the suggestions of Sinn, those Target II transfers would not be possible. And if this 'clearing out' that Sinn proposes had actually taken place before 2012, the biggest losers would have been German and French investors who had flooded the banking and government bond markets.

54 To this category of pro-Grexit voices one should add a number of export-focused capitalists, including those in the tourist industry, and those who possessed considerable wealth outside Greece, who were envisioning returning their money after the depreciation to invest or buy at lower prices.

55 I am deliberately ignoring the crucial issue of the so-called 'migration crisis' of 2015 and the way that Syriza, as a government, dealt with it. The significance and attention that the issue demands does not, unfortunately, fit in this book.

56 The most obvious example concerns the auction of houses of those unable to meet their loan payments. Legislation in 2010 forbade the appropriation of first homes, sensitive to the explosive consequences of implementing such a measure in a country with 87 per cent home ownership. An updated version of the law in 2013 loosened the framework, but retained provisions that allowed debtors to appeal to the courts to delay any appropriation. Research showed that, in most cases, courts reached decisions beneficial to debtors. To counteract this, Syriza has implemented a number of significant

changes: on the one hand, it transformed the legal obligation of protecting first homes to a 'verbal agreement' (between gentlemen, one assumes) on behalf of the banks (not surprisingly, they have not kept their 'word'); on the other hand, it has put pressure on the courts to minimize decisions beneficial to debtors as opposed to the banks: according to reports, only 20–30 per cent of cases are today settled in favour of debtors. As the Troika has made it clear on more than one occasion, the appropriation of houses, which represent toxic loans on bank balance sheets, is the last remaining aspect of austerity that other governments dared not touch, one that is finally on the cards thanks to Syriza's changes. At this moment (December 2017), the topic is creating an explosive atmosphere, representing the first expression of mass discontent against Syriza.

57 These supporters have now placed their perennial hopes for redemption in a new-old saviour of the Left, Labour's Jeremy Corbyn.

58 For reasons of clarity, it would be fair to notice that some mobilizations have taken place. These include a small citizens' movement called 'We Stay in Europe' (*Menoume Europi*), which took to the streets during the referendum days and was eventually transformed into an organization called 'Resign' (Παραιτηθείτε). Its extremely low support can be easily understood by the phenomenal contradiction of its demands: composed of people who have supported the logic of austerity at every step over the last seven years, their 'critique' of Syriza is, at best, surreal, given that Syriza is implementing exactly the type of austerity they consider as necessary. For this reason, their propaganda machine is based on pure nonsense: that Syriza is a Stalinist party that is essentially against investments. More to the point, the core of this 'movement' supports the New Democracy candidate, Kyriakos Mitsotakis, harbouring illusions that he will do a better job with austerity once elected.

## Epilogue: The Future is Not What It Used to Be

1 On top of the absurdity of this plan one should add the systematically wrong projections that the Troika made about the effects of its programmes. I have not come across a single future projection in the Compliance Reports since 2010 (whether it was measuring the deficit, debt, inflation, unemployment or anything else) that was not completely off the mark. To give one example concerning the hot issue of debt/GDP ratio, in 2010 the divergence between the Troika's projections and the actual value was 15 per cent; in 2011 the same divergence was 25.5 per cent; in 2012, 40 per cent, and so on.

2 If one excludes the example of Germany from this wishful thinking, its absurdity becomes even clearer, as it essentially implies the

existence of some correlation between low labour costs and robust economic development. If that were true, then surely the G20 would be made up of sub-Saharan countries.

3   Greek banks were recording high profits while in constant need of recapitalization.

4   This threat was partially dealt with through the PSI agreement in 2012 and essentially ensured by the realization that, no matter what, most Greeks remained in favour of staying inside the Eurozone.

5   The commodity-form and the dictatorship of money are protected but not determined by police repression.

6   The banks and other financial institutions, which, until recently, were the motors of economic 'growth', only use new money created (such as QE and bond purchases) to cover the holes in their balance sheets. The same goes for indebted enterprises in the 'productive' sector. This reversal of the credit machine obstructs the possibility of new investments and, therefore, new profitability.

7   It remains highly indicative that the Left stands outraged by the Right's recalibration of the national narrative to exclude migrants directly, for example, while failing to see that there is no other definition of nationality beyond that of exclusion.

8   Every community (and especially the national one) defines itself through excluding those outside of it. The parliamentary Left does not deny this exclusion but promises to manage it with a 'human face'. A glance at Syriza's record and language during the recent migrant crisis or the UK Labour party's promises of 'controlled migration' is enough to indicate that in today's predicament, even churches appear more progressive than the Left.

# Acknowledgements

The socialization of knowledge has reached such a high degree that 'authors' in fact merely register and revise collectively developed materials, information and reflections, as well as collectively experienced results of practice.

JOHANNES AGNOLI
*Einleitung zu Überlegungen zum bürgerlichen Staat*
(Berlin, 1975)

The above observation by Agnoli makes the task of writing acknowledgements rather difficult. Nonetheless, it would be remiss not to mention my deepest gratitude for those closest to the book. Let me start by stating that this book would not exist were it not for the insistence of Paul Mattick. Paul's tremendously flattering belief in me was a major driving force. Equal respect and gratefulness goes to Vivian Constantinopoulos, Editorial Director of Reaktion Books. Paul's and Vivian's suggestions, editing and crucial remarks greatly improved my initial drafts. I am also deeply indebted to all the staff at Reaktion Books for their tireless efforts and professionalism.

In many ways, this book reflects the (literally) endless discussions that I have had (and continue to do so) with Stathis Stasinos (Techie Chan) and Achilleas Christodoulou. It would be impossible to convey how much I learned from them. My gratitude also extends to John Clegg, Felix Kurz, Jacob Blumenfeld, Steen Thorsson, Giannis Chamodrakas, Evangelia Tombori and Tony Norfield, whose comments, disagreements and insights greatly assisted me in writing this book. Most of all, I cannot thank enough my partner, En, for her amazing patience and unshaken belief in me. Without her, this book would not exist.

Needless to say, I take all the credit for any mistakes and omissions.

# Index